CRYSTAL
chic

CRYSTAL *chic*

Custom jewelry with dazzling details

Debbi Simon

CREATE
YOUR STYLE with
CRYSTALLIZED™
– *Swarovski Elements*

KALMBACH BOOKS

21027 Crossroads Circle
Waukesha, Wisconsin 53186
www.Kalmbach.com/books

All crystals featured in this book
have been sponsored by
CRYSTALLIZED™ – *Swarovski
Elements*

Published in 2008

12 11 10 09 08   1 2 3 4 5

Manufactured in the
United States of America

ISBN: 978-0-87116-269-4

Publisher's Cataloging-in-Publication
Data

Simon, Debbi.   Crystal chic : custom
jewelry with dazzling details / Debbi
Simon.

   p. : ill. ; cm.
   ISBN: 978-0-87116-269-4
   1. Jewelry making--Handbooks,
manuals, etc. 2. Jewelry--Design. 3.
Crystals. I. Title.

TT212 .S56 2008
745.5942

filigree

fibers

metal

contents

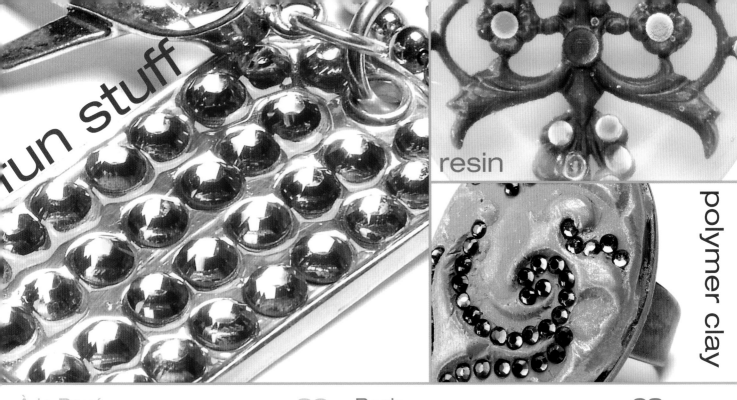

fun stuff

resin

polymer clay

Introduction

Why are crystals so alluring? Is it the unique properties of light and color communicated through these tiny stones? Or, perhaps it's the wide color palette and many finish choices available. As I began to experiment with these faceted gems, I found the interaction of light, hue, and texture dramatically transformed the perception of color in a finished piece. Surprisingly, the same shade in a different shape and size can have a radically different appearance. I quickly realized I could build up beautiful simulated glazes with these stones—as if I was painting with a palette of crystal shapes, sizes, colors, and special finishes.

Crystal Chic explores the many options that working with these beauties presents; you'll find a range of designs and techniques that will lead you to creating one-of-a-kind, dazzling jewelry.

I hope you decide to explore some of the ideas, techniques, or materials presented here. I want you to draw the same conclusion I did: You can make contemporary jewelry that's modern and chic. Be open-minded to the possibilities … and most of all, enjoy!

My Top 10 Favorite Crystals

 Pacific Opal: My all-time favorite crystal color has a pale but warm blue hue. Light on this crystal creates a bravura color reaction.

 Sand Opal: This color has remarkably subtle color shifts. Light reveals hints of many other colors. Try it with opals as well as purples and brighter colors.

 Mocca: Brown is my staple color, so I couldn't be more excited about this shade. Combine it with Pacific or Sand Opal to create a luxurious combination; or for a more surprising grouping, pair it with violet opal.

 Capri Blue: I love this blue! It is so rich and vibrant, but not too bright. Try it with ruby, hyacinth, fuchsia, or citrine.

 Black Diamond: A softer option in the black palette, this color is a subtle accent.

 Tanzanite: Purple was my grandmother's favorite color, and I have always been drawn to purples because of her. Tanzanite gives me the deeper, subtle-but-rich tone I like.

 Amethyst: This is another variation of purple that I like to use.

 Crystal Cosmo Jet: Look carefully for an unexpected hint of blue in the center of the jet black. It complements orange, topaz, and copper nicely.

 Crystal Copper AB: The AB finish adds a trace of cool that plays off the warm copper, creating an altogether different look.

 Padparadsha: I have grown to rely on colors such as ruby, hyacinth, fuchsia, and padparadsha. All have an incomparable color that is as rich as it is bright.

Colors exclusive to CRYSTALLIZED™ – Swarovski Elements

Crystal embellishment is fun, easy, and adds a twist to almost any project. Just like learning anything new, have a little patience, and practice a few times. Before you realize it, you'll be a pro.

Materials and Techniques

It's important to become familiar with some basic materials and techniques that you'll need to make the projects in this book. This section will teach you the basics about glues, flat-back and heat-set crystals, resin casting, and making molds with silicone and polymer clay. You'll also learn a few skills that will help you finish your jewelry. Finally, you'll find an overview of tools and materials called for in the projects. Check with your local bead and craft stores for materials; I've provided specific information for unique items.

All about glue

Because you'll end up gluing most flat-back crystals in place, your finished piece is only as good as the glue that holds it together. Not all glues are created equally. Different glues work in different applications, and different surfaces need different kinds of glue. Begin by reading the label. Here are some quick facts:

• *Two-part epoxy* is recommended because it's easy to use and provides a strong bond. It's formulated for different set-up times including 5, 20, 30, and 60 minutes. The project you're using it for will determine the formula you need. For example, 30-minute epoxy gives you more working time, but 5 minute gives you a quick bond if you're working on a curved surface. Drying time also affects the glue's shrinkage—the faster the drying time, the higher the shrinkage. A fast drying time creates a more brittle bond because the hardened glue is less flexible. Weigh the pros and cons of your choice based on your application. Remember, any epoxy requires a full 24 hours to cure properly.

• *E6000* is an industrial glue that dries clearly and quickly. Many jewelry designers recommend this glue. Its strong odor is unpleasant to some, and the fast drying time can be frustrating. It can also have an adverse effect on some materials; for example, it can lift the foil backings on rhinestones. Follow the manufacturer's safety directions carefully when using this product.

• *Gem Tac* is a popular rhinestone adhesive. It's non-toxic, has no strong odor, and cleans up easily. It can be used to glue crystals onto fabric, wood, plastic, glass, vinyl, and metal. Although Gem Tac is not as strong as two-part epoxy, some designers swear by it and feel the occasional lost stone is worth using this glue.

• Please don't use *cyanoacrylate glues* (instant glues), *any glue with acetone,* or *hot glue*. Instant glues can be brittle, and the bond can break easily if the piece is dropped or exposed to extreme temperatures. Acetone breaks down over time, and hot glue is a quick fix but often loses its bond.

Preparing the surface

A clean surface makes for a secure bond (and is almost as important to your projects' success as the proper glue). Because different surfaces have different properties, consider the following:

• For *metals and glass*, use a degreasing agent, such as rubbing alcohol or acetone, to remove dirt and oils.

• To create a bondable surface on *resin or plastic*, pass a torch flame over the plastic (a kitchen butane torch is fine). If the piece is small, use a lighter or match. This can be dangerous, so make sure you are working in a well-ventilated area and on a non-flammable work surface. Pull long hair back and roll up loose sleeves. Practice on a sample piece first. In a pinch, you can use a baby wipe and immediately dry the piece with a soft cloth. Do not clean resin or plastic with acetone because it can erode the surface.

• Gently sand a *wood* surface with sandpaper. Or if you don't want to ruin the finish, clean with a baby wipe or soft cloth.

tip Letting 30-minute epoxy set or stand for a few minutes before applying crystals helps keep the glue from spreading too much. The epoxy will also be tackier so the stones will not slide around as easily. Keep this in mind if you are working on a curved or dimensional surface.

TOP 10 TIPS Mastering gluing

1. Toothpicks are indispensable. Apply glue, move and arrange crystals, and, best of all, throw them out when the glue builds up.
2. Baby wipes are equally priceless. They keep your tools, hands, and projects clean!
3. Don't use mixed glue once the set time has expired.
4. Always test product compatibility on a sample piece.
5. Try a variety of methods and use what works best for you.
6. Keep fingers, tweezers, and tools clean. Glue residue can leave crystals discolored and cloudy, and can hide the brilliance of the stones.
7. Mix glue on disposable plates.
8. Consult create-your-style.com, the CRYSTALLIZED™ – *Swarovski Elements* Web site. Its design tool is fun to play with, and you'll find product information, including sizes and colors.
9. If you want to know what to glue something with, check out thisto-that.com, Just add this to that and it will do the work for you.
10. Practice and patience...

Mixing and applying glue
Mixing two-part epoxy is easy. Epoxy is sold in a container that dispenses equal amounts of epoxy and hardener. Squeeze out the amount needed and mix completely and evenly with a toothpick or other disposable stick.

Use a tool with a small pointed tip to apply glue. You'll find a favorite through time and experimentation. I've made recommendations based on what I think works best each project.

A toothpick or needle tool is the easiest and most common applicator. What's great about toothpicks is they're abundant and they're disposable. If you choose a needle tool, make sure to wipe off the metal tip as you work so you don't build up dried glue.

A syringe or glue bottle has a small tip and can be used when you need precise placement. To fill, open the top and add adhesive with a toothpick. Let the glue settle to the bottom. Squeeze out the air first over scrap paper until the glue dispenses.

How much glue? The dab of glue should be smaller than the crystal but enough to completely cover the back of stone when it's pushed into the glue. Any gap under the stone creates the risk that something may catch on the stone and pull it off. Too much glue (left) can make a finished piece look messy, and it's hard to clean up! If you add too much glue, you can do one of two things. Remove the crystal, swab the surface with a baby wipe, and reapply, or try to use a cotton swab dipped in acetone to clean around the stone. (This is not my preferred method; it's hard to get consistent results.)

Fill a box or bowl with rice, and you'll have a great place to hold pieces in an upright position while the glue dries and cures. (Sand, small pebbles, or cat litter work, too.)

tip To see if glue will adhere to a surface, mark the surface with ink. If the ink beads, forms droplets, or disappears entirely (top photo), the surface won't bond with glue. If the ink remains (bottom photo), the surface is suitable for gluing. Cleaning, roughing up the surface, or adding primer may help. You can rough up the surface with sandpaper, a flex-shaft tool with a bur bit, or an awl.

All about crystals

Flat-back and hotfix crystals come in many sizes, shapes, and—best of all—colors.

Size

Flat-back crystals are measured in three ways: Stone Size (SS), millimeter (mm), and pearl plate (pp). Stone Size (SS) and millimeter (mm) are most common. You'll see this designation in the materials lists that accompany the projects in this book.

Shape

Round is the most common shape, but there are many interesting shapes to choose from, such as checkerboard squares, flowers, and teardrops.

Color

Crystal colors begin with the familiar and then quickly branch out to many subtle variations. Additionally, coatings—such as Aurora Borealis (AB), Satin, and metallic—alter the original base color. Finishes add a completely new dimension to the existing color palette. Visit the CRYSTALLIZED™ – *Swarovski Elements* Web site, create-your-style.com, to view the range of crystal colors and products available.

Adding and moving crystals

The easiest way to pick up and apply these tiny beauties is with either tweezers or a wax stick. I use both. With a steady hand and a good eye, you'll get the hang of it. And a clean toothpick is indispensable for making adjustments.

Plan your crystal pattern on a flat work surface, placing the crystals pretty side up. Sometimes I apply a light coat of rubber cement on a piece of paper and let it dry. The light tack of the cemented area helps hold crystals in place as I develop my design.

Tweezers

Use tweezers to pick up the crystal, pretty side up. This will take some practice. Carefully carry over and apply to your project.

Wax sticks

A wax stick is a like a toothpick but it has a few layers of beeswax on its point. Pick up the crystal, pretty side up, by touching the wax tip to the top of the crystal. Carefully lift and apply the crystal to the glue. Like tweezers, a wax stick will take some getting used to, and it works better with smaller crystals.

Stone Size (SS) and millimeter (mm) conversion			
SS5	1.8mm	SS16	3.9mm
SS6	2.0mm	SS20	4.7mm
SS7	2.15mm	SS30	6.41mm
SS8	2.35mm	SS34	7.17mm
SS9	2.65mm	SS40	8.54mm
SS10	2.85mm	SS42	9.09mm
SS12	3.1mm	SS48	11.11mm

Art. 2493 Chessboard   Art. 2035   Art. 2483   Art. 2709 Rhombus   Art. 2555 Cosmic Baguette

Art. 21804   Art. 2711   Art. 2300   Art. 2200   Art. 2709 Rhombus   Art. 2610

Art. 2520 Cosmic   Art. 2400   Art. 2028 Xillion Rose   Art. 2510   Art. 2006

Art. 2080   Art. 2029   Art. 2080   Art. 2728   Art. 2072

Work in a well-ventilated area on a protected surface. Follow the manufacturer's directions, set times, and safety precautions.

The first time you mix your glue and start to apply crystals, you will say "Wow … that was easy!"

 **tip**

I prefer CRYSTALLIZED™ – *Swarovski Elements* flat-backed crystals because of their high quality, wide color range, and unique features, such as a 14-facet cut for clarity and brilliance. These crystals are sold at bead, sewing, and craft stores and online. They have a higher lead content than others on the market and therefore more luster.

TOP 10 TIPS — Applying Hotfix Crystals

1. Stones are hot to the touch after application!

2. The hotfix tool can cause serious burns. Use caution and supervision when working with or around children.

3. If your design has many stones in varying sizes, it's helpful to have a separate heating tool for each size.

4. If you have only one tool, try to plan the design so you are applying one size at a time. This strategy keeps you from having to take on and off hot tips continually.

5. Use a thimble or piece of cloth to gently apply pressure to the top of the stone after removing heat tool.

6. If you are having trouble picking up stones with the tool, make the hot tool a little tackier by lightly touching the tip of the tool to the adhesive on an extra stone.

7. Sometimes using a tip one size smaller than the crystal works better.

8. If the stone gets stuck, use a pin or paper clip to pry the stone free.

9. If the glue oozes out around the crystal, the adhesive is too hot.

10. To apply iron-on transfers, heat the fabric with the iron first, and then apply the hotfix motif.

Cleanup

If you need to clean up a glue mishap, such as glue that spread out beneath the stone, is in the wrong place, or you just want to reapply, use a baby wipe.

Drying

Let glue dry completely. Follow manufacturer's recommendations for dry times. Use caution when handling projects before the dry time is complete, including moving on to the next step of the project. All two-part epoxy set times require a full 24 hours to cure completely. Keep this in mind before going on to a step requiring a lot of handling or before wearing the finished piece.

Troubleshooting

Use the most reliable products and application techniques, and you'll ensure the longest possible life of your finished piece with limited repairs. Despite your best efforts, however, you might lose a stone or two. Add some glue and a new crystal to the open spot, and you're set. Stones usually come loose due to an application mistake.

Hotfix stone application

Hotfix stones are similar to flat-back crystals in sizes, shapes, and colors, but offer one major difference: They have a heat-activated adhesive coating that permanently adheres the crystal to most fabrics. CRYSTALLIZED™ – *Swarovski Elements* flat-back hotfix stones have a very strong and reliable adhesive. When proper application instructions are followed, the finished garment can be washed, dried, or dry-cleaned over and over again.

Steps for proper heat setting

Use a tool specifically designed for hotfix crystal application. If the tool is too hot, the adhesive, garment, or even the stone could burn. If it's too cool, it won't heat the adhesive enough to properly adhere the crystal.

1. Following manufacturer's directions, attach the proper size tip to the heat tool. (Various sized attachments that correspond to the varying sizes and shapes of crystals are included with your tool.)

2. Heat the tool for 5–8 minutes.

3. On a flat, heat-resistant surface, place crystals pretty side up. Gently lift stone with the heat tool, and lift the tool and the crystal upright.

4. Let the adhesive heat. This takes about 3–10 seconds, but it will vary depending on the size of stone. The adhesive is ready when it gets glossy and starts to bubble.

5. Quickly turn the tool over and place the stone on the fabric. If the crystal gets stuck in the applicator, slide a pin or paperclip through the slot to remove the stuck crystal.

6. Immediately remove the heat tool so you don't burn the fabric.

7. Apply pressure to the newly affixed crystal. Use something that will protect you from the hot stone, such as a thimble or cloth.

8. After all the crystals are placed, turn the garment or fabric inside out and iron. This helps secure the bond.

Hotfix iron-on transfers

These are easy to apply:

1. Heat iron to 320° (a medium setting without steam).
2. Lay garment or fabric on a flat, heat-resistant surface.
3. Peel the white backing off the hotfix transfer.
4. Lay the transfer down with the adhesive side against the right side of the fabric. Iron directly onto the clear paper until the transfer is adhered to the fabric, about 20–30 seconds. Hold the iron in place; don't move.
5. Let the garment and transfer cool completely, then gently remove the clear paper.

tip To improve adherence, iron the garment before placing a transfer. Heating the fabric before applying the transfer helps activate the adhesive.

To care for the garment, turn it inside out and wash as you normally would. Dry inside out on low heat. If any crystals come loose, run a preheated (320°) iron over the area with crystals and reset the loose crystal(s).

note Hotfix adhesive won't adhere to leather, water-repellent material such as an umbrella, or other materials including metal, ceramic, and wood. The adhesive is made exclusively for fabric; embellished clothing and accessories will withstand washing and normal wear and tear.

tip Lifting the crystals with the tool and releasing them on the fabric takes some getting used to. Practice with extra crystals and scrap fabric.

Make your own transfers

Use clear contact paper to make transfers of your designs:

1. Place crystals on a work surface, pretty side up. Carefully place the sticky side of contact paper directly over the crystals, gently cover, and apply light pressure.
2. Lift the contact paper and turn it over so the backs of the crystals are facing up.
3. Place fabric right-side down on the crystals.
4. Iron with a medium (320°) no-steam setting.
5. Let the fabric and transfer cool completely, then gently remove the clear paper.

Note: This same method can be used for glue-on crystals. Use a syringe to apply a drop of epoxy glue to each crystal. Place fabric as in step 3. Let cure completely before removing the contact paper.

tip Practice and be patient.

All about resin

Resin is a wonderful medium for creating custom jewelry. Here are the basics you'll need to learn before you attempt the projects in the resin chapter.

You will need:
Two-part casting resin
Disposable measuring cups
Wooden stick for mixing
Parchment paper
Bottle and syringe top

Protect your surface: I usually use parchment paper to protect the area I'm working on. Parchment paper makes a good disposable surface that resin doesn't stick to. Work in a well-ventilated area, and always read the label so you can follow the manufacturer's safety information.

Follow these easy steps for success:
1. Trace over the lines on the measuring cup with a marker to make it easier to see the lines.
2. Add resin to the second line, following manufacturer's directions (usually a 1:1 ratio). Be as precise as possible in your measurements. If you have more resin than hardener, the resin will not cure completely.
3. Mix the two parts by slowly folding into one another with a stir stick. Make sure that you scrape the sides of the measuring cup and stick as you are mixing. This ensures both parts are equally distributed and minimizes air bubbles. Mix for about a minute. Let it stand for a minute and then mix a few more times before casting into molds. The batch will be workable for about 45 minutes. When the resin expires, dispose of the excess, the stir stick, the measuring cup, and any applicators or containers used. Never reuse to mix a new batch or you could contaminate the new batch.
4. Let pieces sit in an undisturbed area while curing.

tip Temperature and humidity can affect the success of your finished piece. Place your object under a warm light to keep it warm and dry while it's curing.

All about molds

Making your own molds increases your creative control and ensures your project will be unique. My favorite ways to make molds are with two-part silicone and with polymer clay.

Two-part silicone mold
A two-part silicone mold is easy to use, and almost any material can be used to make a mold without damage. When the silicone mold is cured, it's flexible, so it's very easy to remove a cast piece.

1. Measure two equals parts of part A silicone and B hardener.
2. Following manufacturer's directions, knead the two parts together. You will need to work fast because the working time is limited (Curing times might differ from product to product. Refer to manufacturer's directions).
3. Continue to mix the two compounds until the marble pattern becomes a solid color. Once all marbling is kneaded to an even color, the compound is mixed and will start to cure.
4. Roll the compound into a ball and push an item into the ball of silicon. Let set completely.
5. Remove the item from the mold and you are ready to cast.

Polymer Clay
An inexpensive and readily available material at craft and art stores, polymer clay can be used to make molds. However, it becomes hard after baking, so it can be difficult to remove castings. For simple and not very detailed molds, it is a great alternative to silicon.

1. Knead the unbaked clay until it is soft. Roll into a ball and push an object into the clay.
2. Place in refrigerator or freezer a few minutes. This step will firm the clay a little, making it easier to remove the object without compromising the mold.
3. Remove the object from the mold. Return the clay to room temperature.
4. Follow manufacturer's direction's to bake, (usually 275° and 15 minutes for each ¼-in. thickness). The clay should be hard but still a little flexible.
5. Once your mold has cooled, you are ready to cast.

Basic jewelry and beading techniques

Opening and closing jump rings
1. Using two pairs of chainnose pliers, position one on each side of the jump ring's opening.
2. Bring one pair of pliers toward you and push the other away from you. (Never pull apart from side to side. This will weaken the wire and make it hard to close into a neat ring.)
3. Reverse the steps to close the open ring.

Making a loop
1. Trim wire or a head pin ⅜-in. (1cm) from the end.
2. Use roundnose pliers to grab wire at the tip. Gently bend the wire around the roundnose pliers to start the loop.
3. Reposition the roundnose pliers and continue bending until you have a complete loop.
4–5. Reposition the roundnose pliers at the stem of the loop and gently bend back. Turn slightly to close and shape the loop.

Making a wrapped loop
1. On wire or a head pin, use roundnose pliers to grab wire directly above an object. Bend the wire over the pliers.
2. Reposition the roundnose pliers in the bend. Bend the wire around the pliers.
3. Reposition the pliers so that the bottom jaw is in the loop. With chainnose pliers, grab the tail of wire and pull wire tightly around the stem two to four times to fill the gap. Pull tightly and wrap carefully, following the stem to make a neat coil.
4. Trim the excess wire and gently use chainnose pliers to press the cut end down into the coil.

Crimping
1. Thread a crimp bead on one end of the strung piece, add the finishing finding, and thread the wire back through the crimp bead. Using the first hole (or the hole with notch) on the crimping pliers, place it directly over the crimp bead. Holding the wires apart, squeeze the pliers to compress the crimp bead.
2. Reposition the pliers to place the compressed crimp bead in the first hole. Position the flattened crimp bead on its side so the dent is facing outward. Squeeze the tool to fold the crimp in half.
3. Check to make sure the crimp is secure.

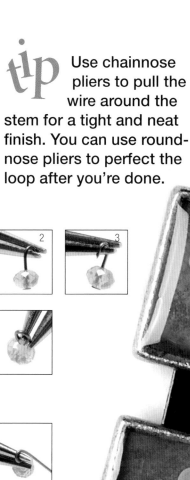

tip Use chainnose pliers to pull the wire around the stem for a tight and neat finish. You can use round-nose pliers to perfect the loop after you're done.

My favorite tools:

Chainnose pliers are usually used in pairs to open and close jump rings. If you need one, you should have two.

Fine wire cutters should be reserved for 20-gauge or higher (thinner) wire to protect the blades.

A syringe dispenses only a small amount of glue.

Roundnose pliers are essential for making wire loops.

Flush cutters or heavy-duty wire cutters are perfect for cutting harder wire and base metal forms.

A toothpick is my favorite tool; it is indispensable for doing the projects in this book. I keep many on hand and toss them when they are used.

A needle tool is used in place of a toothpick, but remember, it's not disposable.

A wax stick is another useful tool for picking up rhinestones.

Tweezers are perfect for picking up tiny beads.

My most commonly used materials:

Two-part epoxy glue, (5, 10, 15, and 30 min.)
Findings
Carbon transfer paper
Clear contact paper
Craft paint
Decoupage medium
Embossing powders
Epoxy Resin
Ferido Glue Putty
G-S Hypo Cement
Judi-kins Amazing Glaze
Liver of sulfur
Molds
Parchment paper
Polymer clay
Polymer glaze

My other favorites:

Disposable foam brush
Craft knife
Hole punch
Hotfix tool
Ring mandrel
Rubber stamps
Ruler
Sand paper

Scissors
Self-healing cutting surface
Small containers
Small rolling pin exclusive for clay
Sponge or sponge brush

Filigree is ornamental open-work, usually of fine silver or gold, in a lacy design. Patterns often contain scrolls and arabesques. In recent years, filigree has had a strong showing. Modern stampings made of a variety of metals are widely available. Designs are both vintage and contemporary. Some are modern twists on an old theme, and others are reproductions made from original metal stamps. My joy in designing with filigree comes from bending, wrapping, cutting, or altering the original form and then— adding crystals!

Filigree

Ring on a Shoestring

Wrap these metal filigree stampings to your size for super-fabulous rings. Choose vintage style or keep it whimsical; these are so easy to make, you can do both!

Crystals
Version I (above, center)
2 SS12 Art. 2028, Dorado
7 SS10 Art. 2028, Jet Black
5 SS8 Art. 2028, Black Diamond
4 SS6 Art. 2028, Black Diamond

Version II (above, left)
13 x 8mm Art. 2709, Crystal AB
2 SS16 Art. 2728, Crystal AB

Version III (above, right):
10 x 6mm Art. 2709, Crystal
   Golden Shadow
2 SS10 Art. 2028, Pacific Opal
8 SS8 Art. 2028, Pacific Opal

Materials
47 x 35mm brass Art Deco
   dragonfly pendant or
   64 x 21mm brass diamond
   trellis filigree wrap (Vintaj
   Natural Brass Co., vintaj.com)
two-part epoxy glue (30 min.)

Tools
ring mandrel
chainnose pliers
roundnose pliers
tweezers
toothpick or syringe

Shape the rings
Version I
1. Using roundnose pliers, gently start to bend the dragonfly's wing (**a**).
2. Align the bent wing with your ring size on the mandrel (**b**).
3. Continue bending the form until the stamping is completely curved around the mandrel. Remove.

Versions II and III
1. Using roundnose pliers, gently start to bend one end of the filigree form.
2. Align the bent form with your ring size on the mandrel (**c**).
3. Continue bending until the form is completely curved around the mandrel. Remove.

Add crystals
1. Mix epoxy (Basics). Use either a toothpick or a syringe to apply glue to the ring form (**d**). Add crystals in the pattern of your choice (**e**).
2. Stabilize the finished ring in a container of uncooked rice to dry (**f**).

a

b

c

d

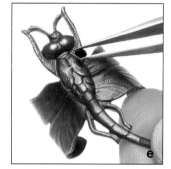
e

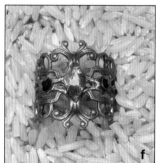
f

tip Small metal charms are an unexpected addition. Glue charms with two-part epoxy just as you did with the crystals.

Fil-harmonic

Orchestrate metal filigree and chain into these glamorous earrings, and dress up your evening with their brilliant sparkle. The result is truly music to your ears!

Version I

- 2 8 x 6mm fancy stones, Art. 4320 Pacific Opal
- 2 SS10 Art. 2028, Pacific Opal
- 2 brass 25 x 33mm Fanned Trellis (Vintaj Natural Brass Co., vintaj.com)
- 2 brass ear wires (Vintaj Natural Brass Co.)

Version II

- 6 SS10 Art. 2028 Aquamarine Cosmo Jet
- 12 SS10 Art. 2028 Crystal Golden Shadow
- 2 brass 26 x 55mm Etruscan Drop (Vintaj Natural Brass Co.)
- 9 in. (23cm) 2mm gunmetal chain
- 2 brass ear wires (Vintaj Natural Brass Co.)

Version III

- 2 SS34 Art. 2028, Crystal Meridan Blue
- 2 silver tiny fleur-de-lis drops, F235-AS (Jewels n Findings, jewelsnfindings.com)
- 2 silver openwork drop settings, F381-AS (Jewels n Findings)
- 2 bezels
- 2 2mm silver jump rings
- 2 silver ear wires

Tools

- chainnose pliers
- roundnose pliers
- two-part epoxy glue (30 min.)
- toothpick
- syringe (optional)
- tweezers

Version I
Pacific Opal

1. With the back side of the filigree form up, bend the form toward you with roundnose pliers (**a**). Repeat on opposite edge to create a setting.

2. Place the fancy stone in the setting with the back facing you (**b**).

3. Use chainnose pliers to turn the edges and secure the stone in the setting (**c**).

4. Mix epoxy (Basics). Use a toothpick to apply glue to the front of the filigree form. Add the 2028 crystal (**d**). Let dry.

5. Open an earring wire (Basics) and attach the dangle (**e**). Close the earring wire. Make a second earring to match the first.

Version II
Chain enhanced

1. Cut two 2¼-in. (5.7cm) and two 2-in. (5cm) lengths of chain. Set aside.

2. Mix epoxy (Basics). Use a toothpick to apply glue to the back of the filigree form where the chain will hang. Use tweezers to attach a longer chain length to the top dab of glue on each side, and a shorter length to the bottom on each side (**f**). Let dry.

3. Mix epoxy. Use either a toothpick or a syringe to apply glue to the front of the filigree form where the crystals will be placed. Apply the crystals.

4. Open an earring wire (Basics) and attach the dangle. Close the earring wire. Make a second earring to match the first.

Version III
Silver filigree

1. Mix epoxy (Basics). Use either a toothpick or a syringe to apply glue to two bezels. Add a crystal to each bezel (**g**).

2. Glue the bezel to the larger filigree form with epoxy (**h**). Let dry completely.

3. Attach the small filigree dangle (**i**) with a 2mm jump ring.

4. Open an earring wire (Basics) and attach the dangle (**j**). Close the earring wire. Make a second earring to match the first.

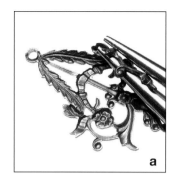

a

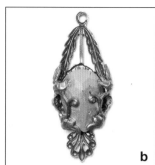

b

c

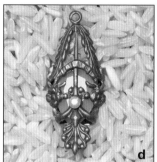

d

e

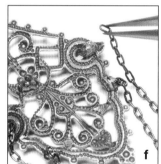

f

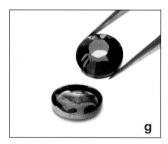

g

h

i

j

Filigree Squared

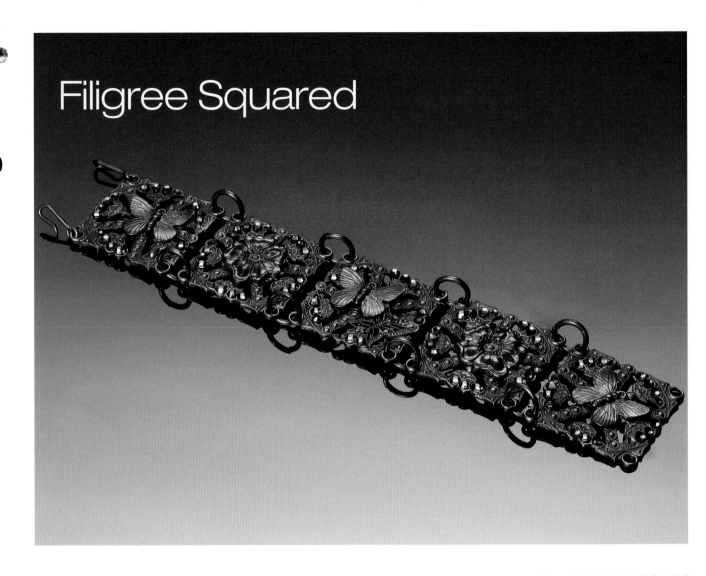

Metallic paints are all you need to create the look of timeworn patina. Crystals add the finishing touch and a burst of color to this linked bracelet.

Crystals
antiqued version
- 80 SS10 flat back crystals, 20 in each of 4 colors

silver linked version
- 7 10mm Art. 2072, Rose Alabaster

Materials
antiqued version
- all stampings are from Vintaj Natural Brass Co., vintaj.com.
- 2 flower metal stampings
- 3 butterfly (a) metal stampings
- 1 butterfly (b) metal stamping

- 3 colors of acrylic metallic paint (I used Plaid Metallic Sapphire Blue, Metallic Antique Copper, and Metallic Amethyst)
- 5 or 6 32 x 32mm Etruscan Kaleidoscope Pendants
- 8–10 8mm jump rings
- 2 6mm hook clasps
- two-part epoxy glue (30 min.)

silver linked version
- 7 9mm fancy settings (F341-AS Jewels n Findings, jewelsnfindings.com)

- 8 metal stampings, (F156 Jewels n Findings)
- end connector bar (Jewels n Findings)
- 14 8mm jump rings
- 3 6mm jump rings
- toggle clasp half
- two-part epoxy glue (30 min.)

Tools
- flush cutters or heavy-duty wire cutters
- toothpick
- tweezers
- paintbrush
- metal file, optional

tip For the pink-and-silver version, glue the bezels to the filigree and then glue the crystals in the center. The toggle connects to an open filigree for a unique clasp.

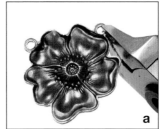

tip Don't use your good wire cutters to trim or cut filigree. The metal is hard and may ruin your cutters. Use basic flush or heavy-duty wire cutters and reserve your good cutters for finer wire … you'll be thankful you did! (Take it from someone who ruined an expensive pair.)

Prepare the components

1. Select metal charms and trim any loops with flush cutters (**a**). Use a metal file to sand the rough edges left after trimming the metal charms.

2. Create a patina effect by painting colors in layers on the front of the charm (**b**). When you're happy with the effect, set the charm aside to dry for an hour or follow the manufacturer's instructions. Repeat with remaining charms.

3. Mix epoxy (Basics). Apply epoxy to the back of the painted charm, filling any grooves and building up the glue as you go. Place the filigree on a flat surface and glue the charm to the top of the filigree (**c**). Set aside to dry. Repeat on all forms. Let dry overnight before proceeding to the next step.

Add crystals

4. On a flat surface, plan a crystal pattern pretty side up.

5. Mix epoxy (Basics). Use either a toothpick or a syringe to apply glue to the front of the first form, following the planned pattern. Apply glue to three of the five forms (**d**).

6. Add crystals to the glue (**e**). Let the glue set a little to help keep the crystals from sliding. Repeat pattern on all three forms.

7. Repeat steps 2–3 to finish the last two forms. Set all aside to dry completely (overnight is best).

Finish the bracelet

8. Plan the bracelet by arranging the forms on your workspace. Connect all filigree shapes with 8mm jump rings (Basics) (**f**).

9. Add a hook to one side of the bracelet by opening its loop and attaching it to the filigree form (**g**). Close the loop. Repeat with a second hook.

tip Plan your pattern and arrange crystals on your work surface before you mix and apply the glue to help maximize your working time.

Full Circle

Pacific Opal is one of my favorite colors because the blue is cool yet the warmth of the infused opal shines through. It's particularly stunning with antiqued brass.

Crystals
12mm fancy stone Art. 4470, Pacific Opal
4 SS12 Art. 2028, Pacific Opal
8 SS8 Art. 2028, Pacific Opal

Materials
49 x 49mm brass princess-cut filigree wrap
49mm brass ornate wreath filigree wrap
26 in. (66cm) 6.5 x 9.5mm brass etched-cable chain
26 in. (66cm) 10mm brass round-link chain
26 in. (66cm) 3.5 x 4mm brass cable chain
6 8mm brass jump rings
2–6 3mm brass jump rings
3-in. (7.6cm) brass head pin
22mm brass hammered ring
6 x 30mm brass engraved oval toggle bar
two-part epoxy glue (30 min.)
Renaissance Wax (optional)

supply note: brass components are from Vintaj Natural Brass Co., vintaj.com.

Tools
flush cutters
2 pairs chainnose pliers
roundnose pliers
ruler
tweezers
toothpick

Make the pendant

1. With the front side of the square filigree up, bend a corner up 45 degrees (**a**). Repeat on all corners.

2. Set the fancy stone in the center (**b**). (If you'd like, use a dab of epoxy to secure the stone.)

3. Place the round form face-up on top of the altered square form. With chainnose pliers, bend the corners down, flattening the filigree square and securing the two forms together (**c**).

4. Mix epoxy (Basics). Using a toothpick or syringe, dab glue on the front of the pendant (where you'd like to place the crystal pattern). Let the glue set for a few minutes and then add the crystals.

Add the chain

5. Cut the etched-cable chain and the round-link chain into 14½-in. and 6-in. (36.8cm/15cm) lengths. Cut the plain cable chain into 18-in. and 10-in. (46/25cm) lengths.

6. With the pendant facing up, open and link an 8mm jump ring (Basics) to the left upper side of pendant (**d**). Link the longer lengths of the etched-cable and round-link chain to the open jump ring (**e**). Close the jump ring.

7. Open an 8mm jump ring and link it to the bottom left side of the pendant. Attach the longer length of the brass cable chain to the open jump ring (**f**). Close the jump ring.

8. Attach the remaining lengths of chain to the right side of the pendant, reversing the order by attaching the etched-cable chain to the top jump ring. Close the jump ring. On the lower jump ring, attach the round-link and brass cable chain. Close the jump ring.

Finish the necklace

9. Make a toggle by stringing the bar onto a head pin (**g**). Make a wrapped loop (Basics) above the bar and trim excess wire.

10. Open an 8mm jump ring and attach three lengths of chain to the loop above the toggle (**h**). Close the jump ring.

11. Repeat on the other side, substituting a hammered ring for the toggle bar.

Drape the chain

12. Focusing on one side, lay out the necklace and plan where you'd like to link the chain together to create a pleasing drape (**i**).

13. Open one or more 3mm jump rings, attach the chain where you'd like, and close the jump rings. Repeat on the other side.

14. After all the chain is secure, hold up the necklace to your neckline and adjust if necessary.

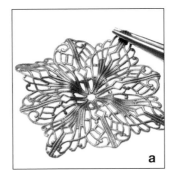
a

b

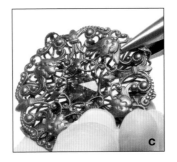
c

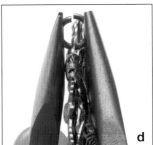
d

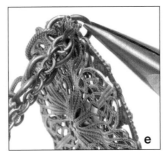
e

f

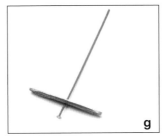
g

h

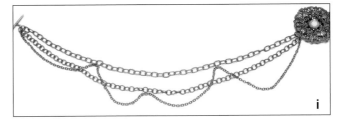
i

tip

Manipulating metal with pliers can nick the finish. Coat these areas with Renaissance Wax to help protect the exposed areas from rusting and to enhance the finish and keep it looking its best.

Checkmate

Use these faceted crystal squares to make dazzling components for a bold necklace. Wearing this, you'll be sure of your next move.

Crystals (all chessboard crystals Art. 2493)
4 10mm, Crystal Silver Shade
2 12mm, Crystal
1 20mm, Crystal

Materials
18 12mm oval brass filigree beads
7 clear rubber ear nuts
7 aluminum bails (JP Designs, coolartwear.com)
flexible beading wire, .018 or .019
2 2mm crimp beads

12 in. (30cm) brass chain
2 6mm brass jump rings
brass lobster claw clasp
two-part epoxy glue (5 min.)

Tools
crimping pliers
2 pairs chainnose pliers
craft knife
syringe or toothpick

Prepare the bails

1. Trim the sides of a rubber ear nut to fit into the back of a bail (**a**), and position it in the bail. This will help prevent the heavy crystal from dropping or turning around. Repeat with the remaining ear nuts and bails.

2. Mix two-part epoxy (Basics). Use a toothpick or a syringe to apply glue to the front of an aluminum bail. Line up the chessboard crystal, place on the bail, and apply light pressure for a few minutes until set (**b**). Place component upright in a container of rice to let dry completely. Repeat with remaining crystals and bails. Set aside and dry completely (overnight is best).

Finish the necklace

3. Plan the pattern of crystals and beads on a bead board and string the pattern, leaving about 6 in. (15cm) of wire on each end (**c**). My pattern is three 12mm beads, a 10mm crystal unit, two 12mm beads, a 12mm crystal unit, two 12mm beads, a 10mm crystal unit, two 12mm beads, and the 20mm crystal unit. It repeats in the mirror image on the other side of the 20mm unit.

4. String a crimp bead onto one end of the beading wire, thread through an end link of chain, and go back through the crimp bead and a few more beads. Crimp the bead and trim the wire (Basics) (**d**).

5. Open a jump ring (Basics) and attach the chain end and lobster claw clasp. Close the jump ring (**e**).

6. On the other end of the necklace, string a crimp bead and a jump ring onto the beading wire, and go back through the crimp bead and a few more beads. Tighten the wire, crimp the crimp bead, and trim the excess wire.

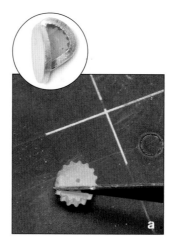

a

b

c

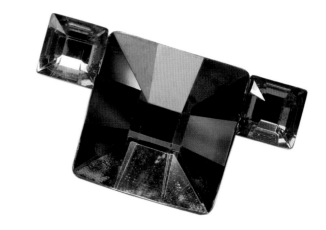

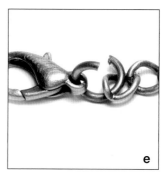

d

e

tip Affordable and versatile, rubber bead bumpers and earring stoppers (or ear nuts) can be very useful. They help keep beads in place and secure heavier flat stones, stopping them from turning. Be innovative when using these rubber findings to engineer your designs!

Fil-osophical

Don't get too philosophical—over-thinking will take away from the simplicity of this bangle. The metal and wood create a serene and peaceful union.

tip You'll need to hold the filigree in place as the glue sets, so use five-minute epoxy. You may need to mix small batches as you add crystals in the later steps.

Crystals
10mm Art. 2072, Rose Alabaster
8 SS12 Art. 2028, Mint Alabaster
16 SS10 Art. 2028, Rose Alabaster

Materials
42mm brass round passion-flower petal filigree (Vintaj Natural Brass Co., vintaj.com)
wood bangle bracelet
two-part epoxy glue (5 min.)

Tools
chainnose pliers
tweezers
toothpick

Form the filigree
1. Use chainnose pliers to slightly bend the petals of the filigree form (**a**). Repeat with all petals. Place the flower on the bangle and check the fit. Adjust if necessary by bending the petals.
2. Mix epoxy (Basics). With a toothpick, dab the glue to the center back of the flower pendant and on all petal tips (**b**).
3. Position the flower filigree on the bangle and gently hold until the glue sets.

Add crystals
4. Mix epoxy. Dab glue with a toothpick in the center of flower filigree. Let set for a minute, then add the 10mm crystal. Let dry.
5. Glue SS10 crystals around the center crystal. Let dry.
6. Glue SS12 crystals around the circle of crystals. Let dry.

a

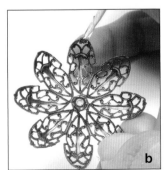

b

Metal

Metal is a perennial jewelry-designer's darling. Sterling silver will always be popular, but base metal alternatives are gaining appeal. There are many great metal components available in a wide range of finishes—including gunmetal, antiqued copper, and oxidized silver—so it's even easier to be creative. Don't be afraid to mix or match!

Ring Around the Posy

A pocketful of flowers celebrates summer no matter what the season. Stack a few or wear a single ring to showcase a single bloom.

Crystals (all Art. 2028)
To make all the rings pictured
above, I used:
8 SS3 Crystal
9 SS5 Purple Velvet
25 SS6 Amethyst
7 SS6 Lt. Amethyst
56 SS6 Citron
8 SS10 Smoked topaz
8 SS10 Aquamarine
9 SS10 Amethyst
6 SS10 Topaz
9 SS10 Tanzanite
6 SS10 Lt. Amethyst
8 3mm round crystals, any color

Materials
for one ring with three flowers:
silver or gold brad assortment
  "small fancy flowers" (Decorative Details/NunnDesign
  nunndesign.com)
plain stackable ring (Shiana,
  Shiana.com)
3 2-in. (5cm) head pins
two-part epoxy glue (30 min.)

Tools
syringe
tweezers
toothpick
chainnose pliers
roundnose pliers
flush cutters

Prepare the flowers

1. Choose three metal flower forms from the assortment (**a**).

2. Plan a pretty-side-up crystal pattern on a flat surface for each flower. Mix epoxy (Basics). Use either a toothpick or a syringe to apply glue to the front of a flower form where you'd like the crystals. Repeat with the remaining forms.

3. Add crystals to the flowers in the order in which you applied the glue (**b**). (Letting the glue set a little will help keep crystals from sliding around.) Repeat to finish remaining flowers. Set aside and let dry completely (overnight is best).

Make the ring

4. String a 3mm crystal and a flower onto a head pin (**c**).

5. Make the first half of a wrapped loop (Basics). Slide the ring's loop onto the head pin (**d**) and complete the wrap.

6. Repeat with the remaining flowers.

7. Mix a second batch of epoxy. Use either a toothpick or a syringe to apply glue to the end of the head pins. Let the glue set and add a crystal. Repeat with remaining flowers. Let dry completely.

a

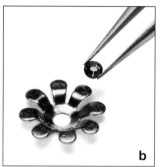

b

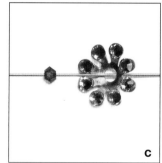

c

d

tip

Substitute contemporary or vintage Lucite flowers for the metal forms. Choices are abundant; Beadin' Path and Gail Crossman-Moore have great Lucite flowers.

No-Hassle Tassel

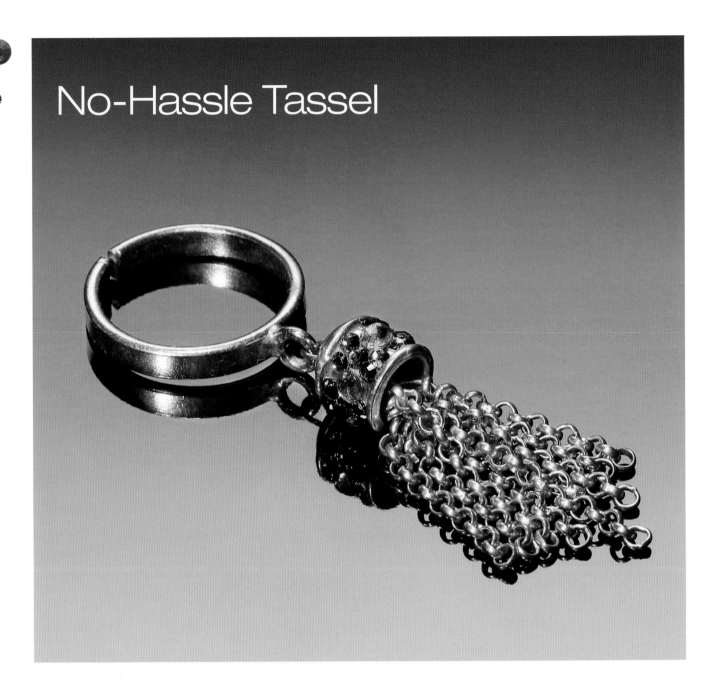

Gold has always been a sign of opulence and wealth. Create a regal tassel ring—made even more distinctive with a palette of pleasing crystals.

Crystals (all Art. 2028)
20 SS5, Purple Velvet
5 SS8, Caribbean Blue
5 SS10, Topaz

Materials
5–10mm vermeil bead cap
10 in. (25cm) 3mm gold-filled
   cable chain
4mm gold-filled jump ring
2½-in. (6.4cm) gold-filled wire
vermeil stackable ring
   (Shiana, shiana.com)
two-part epoxy glue (30 min.)

Tools
syringe
tweezers
toothpick
2 pairs chainnose pliers
roundnose pliers
flush cutters

tip

For a quicker version, buy ready-made eight-strand chain tassels and trim chain (Rings & Things, rings-things.com).

Prepare the tassel

1. Cut 8–10 1-in. (2.5cm) chain lengths. Open a jump ring (Basics) and attach the chain lengths (**a**). Close the jump ring.

2. Make the first half of a wrapped loop at the end of the wire (Basics). Attach the jump ring with chain to the loop, finish the wraps, and string the bead cap (**b**).

Make the ring

3. Trim the wire to ⅜ in. (1cm). Make a plain loop (Basics) above the cap (**c**).

4. Open the loop and link the ring's loop (**d**). Close the loop.

5. Trim the ends of the chain so they are even (**e**).

Add the crystals

6. Mix epoxy (Basics). Use a toothpick or a syringe to apply glue to the bead cap. Add crystals with tweezers or wax stick as you go (**f**). Repeat around the cap. Set aside and let dry completely (overnight is best).

note Vermeil, pronounced *vehr-MAY*, is heavily plated (24K) gold over sterling silver.

a

b

c

d

e

f

4x the Fun

Mix and match these distinctively different designs. Pair them, bunch them, or single one out for a versatile fashion statement.

Crystals
30–50 SS8 Art. 2028 Olivine
30–50 SS8 Art. 2028 Khaki
20–30 SS6 Art. 2028 Purple
  Velvet
25mm Topaz
2–3 10–25mm Art. 2483
  Peridot
10mm Art. 2483 Aquamarine
10mm Art. 2483 Topaz
20mm Art. 2493 Aquamarine
20mm Art. 2493 Light Rose
20mm Art. 2493 Black Diamond
20mm Art. 2035 Peridot
30mm Art. 2035 Aquamarine
16mm Art. 2006 Crystal

Materials
28–33 6–12mm pearls
4 metal forms
rub-on transfer
12 in. (30cm) 24-gauge half-hard
  wire
20 in. (51cm) 22-gauge silver
  wire
20 5mm jump rings
52 in. (1.3m) 2 x 4mm cable
  chain
104 in. (2.6m) 1 x 2mm cable
  chain
4 6mm snap clasps
two-part epoxy glue (30 min.)
spray varnish

Tools
chainnose pliers
roundnose pliers
flush cutters
craft stick
toothpick or syringe

Pearl necklaces

1. Select enough pearls to make four combinations of 2–5 beads each. (It's interesting if you vary the size, quantity, and color of pearls in your units.)

2. On a spare head pin or wire scrap, string a pearl and bend the wire slightly to hold the pearl in place at the halfway point. (This will help stabilize the pearl during the next steps.)

3. Mix epoxy (Basics). Use a toothpick or a syringe to apply glue to the areas on the pearl where you would like to add crystals. Repeat on 3–5 pearls. (At least one of the pearls per unit should have crystals.) Put aside to dry.

4. Burnish a rub-on transfer on as many of the remaining pearls (**a**) as you'd like. Coat with spray varnish to protect. Set aside.

5. Cut a 4-in. (10cm) piece of wire. Make the first half of a wrapped loop on one end. Add a pearl pattern. (To make your design more appealing, vary the pattern of pearls on each unit.) Make the first half of a wrapped loop on the other end (**b**). Set aside. Repeat to make a total of three pearl units.

6. Cut each chain length in half. (Reserve the second half of each of the chain lengths for the metal form necklaces.)

7. Cut one chain in two random places. Attach an end of a chain piece to an end of a pearl unit and complete the wraps (**c**). Repeat with a second chain segment and the other end of the pearl unit.

8. Open a jump ring (Basics) and attach the end link of a chain segment and half of a snap clasp (**d**). Repeat on the other end with the remaining clasp half.

9. Cut the remaining chain from Step 6 in half. Repeat Steps 7–8. When you make the random cuts in Step 7, do it in the same place on each half.

10. Make a second necklace similar to the first.

Metal form necklaces

1. Select enough metal forms (**e**) to make four combinations. Vary the size and shape of the metal forms for interest.

2. Mix epoxy (Basics). Using a toothpick, apply glue to the area on the metal form where you plan to add crystals. Add crystals, varying the design as you did in the pearl versions (**f**). (Be bold with your choices! I used larger square and circle crystals to contrast with the pearls). Put aside to dry. Repeat on all forms.

3. Cut the reserved chain lengths in half. Link crystal units and chain as you did before, substituting jump rings for the wire.

4. Repeat Step 8 of the pearl project to attach a clasp.

5. Make a second necklace similar to the first.

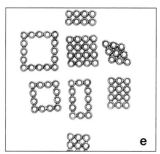

On (Head) Pins and Needles

Copper's appeal is often its time-worn patina. Adding bright blue crystals is a quicker way to get the look.

Crystals (all Art. 2028)
6 SS10 color A, Tanzanite
6 SS10 color B, Citron
6 SS10 color C, Topaz
6 SS10 color D, Fuchsia
6 SS10 color E, Capri Blue
6 SS6 color F, Blue Zircon
6 SS6 color G, Citron
6 SS6 color H, Olivine
6 SS6 color I, Purple Velvet
2 SS6 color J, Ruby
3 2mm Art. 5000, Lt. Colorado Topaz
3 2mm Art. 5000, Tanzanite

Materials
18–22mm 3-strand screen box clasp, copper (Ornamentea, ornamentea.com)
60 1-in. (2.5cm) copper head pins
54 in. 3mm cable chain, copper
6 5mm jump rings
22-gauge half-hard wire
two-part epoxy glue (30 min.)
cotton ball

Tools
tweezers
toothpick
chainnose pliers
roundnose pliers
flush cutters

Prepare the crystal headpins

1. Mix epoxy (Basics). Glue a SS10 crystal to the flat end of each of 30 headpins using six each of color A, B, C, D, and E. These become the flower petals. (**a**, **b**) Set in a foam plate to dry (**c**).

2. On the flat end of each of 18 head pins, glue a SS6 crystal, using six each of color F, G, and H. These become the grasses. Set in a foam plate to dry.

3. On the flat end of each of six head pins, glue a SS6 crystal, using one each of color F, G, H, and I, and two of J. These become the flower centers. Set in a foam plate to dry.

Assemble the mesh clasp

4. Place six color A head pins and one head pin from Step 3 in the center of the mesh. Gather the ends under the mesh form and wrap wire around the group, close to the mesh form (**d**).

5. Mix epoxy (Basics). Glue the head pins just above the top of the wire wrap. Let the glue set. Trim excess ends off head pins.

6. Repeat Steps 4 and 5 with remaining colors B ,C, D and E.

7. Place a head pin from Step 3 through an open hole in the mesh, and make a loop. With chainnose pliers, bend loop up to a right angle (**e**).

Finish the necklace

8. Cut copper chain into three 18-in. (46cm) lengths. With 5mm jump rings, attach each chain end to a clasp loop (**f**). Repeat with the other clasp half (**g**).

9. Fill the bottom of the clasp with cotton.

10. Place the mesh form (with the head pins snug to the top) on top of the bottom form. (The cotton helps hold the head pins and keeps them from moving around too much, although a little movement is good.) Using chainnose pliers, bend the tabs to secure the mesh form to the clasp (**h**).

Once I realized how versatile mesh findings are, they quickly became one of my design favorites. Treat filigree lacework much the same way.

a

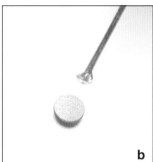

b

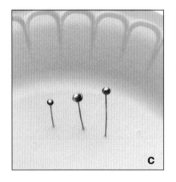

c

d

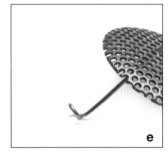

e

f

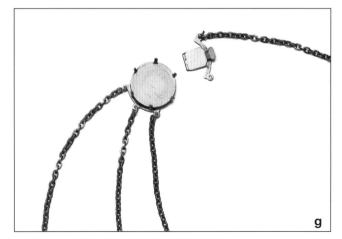

g

h

À la Pavé

Pavé has a sophisticated appeal. Now you can simulate the look without expert metal-smithing skills or the expensive price tag. No one will know how easy it is.

Ring Version
Crystals (all Art. 2028)
65 SS3 Crystal
13 SS6 Purple Velvet
13 SS6 Citrine
3 SS10 Topaz
3 SS10 Tanzanite
3 SS10 Amethyst
3 SS10 Light Amethyst

Materials
6mm silver channel ring
   (Rio Grande, riogrande.com)
Ferido glue putty kit, clear
   (Gesswein, gesswein.com)

Clasp Version
Crystals (all Art. 2028)
10 SS3 Crystal
15 SS10 Smoked Topaz
20 SS8 Smoked Topaz
15 SS10 Olivine
20 SS8 Olivine

Materials
small silver bezel clasp
   (Susan Lenart Kazmer,
   susanlenartkazmer.net)
Ferido glue putty kit, clear
   (gesswein.com)
4 fold-over crimps

3 large-hole spacers
5mm jump ring
20 in. (51cm) medium leather
   cord, black
two-part epoxy glue (5 min.)

Tools (both projects)
tweezers
toothpick
scissors

Make the ring

1. On a flat surface, lay out crystal pattern pretty side up.
2. Mix Ferido epoxy putty, following the manufacturer's directions. You'll have about 45 minutes of working time before the putty hardens.
3. Add a thin layer of mixed putty to the ring's channel cut (**a**). Spread putty until the entire channel is full. With your fingers, smooth the putty until the surface is even.
4. Place crystals (**b**). Continue until you meet the starting point. (Depending on your ring size, you may need to make adjustments as needed to transition to your starting point.)
5. Set aside and let the putty set completely.

Make the bezel clasp

1. On a flat surface, place crystals pretty side up.
2. Mix Ferido epoxy putty, following the manufacturer's directions. You'll have about 45 minutes of working time before the putty hardens.
3. Fill bezel with putty until almost full. With your fingers, smooth the putty until the surface is even.
4. Beginning with SS10 crystals, make a circle in the center (**c**). Moving outward, add the same color SS8 around the inner circle. Continue adding crystals, moving outward and alternating with SS10 and SS8. Continue until the bezel is filled (**d**). Use the SS3 crystals to fill spaces on the outside edge.
5. Set the clasp aside until the putty sets completely.

Make the bracelet

1. Decide on the size of your bracelet, cut a piece of cord four times that length (7 in. x 4 = 28 in.), and cut in half.
2. On one of the cords, add a crimp end, secure with a dab of glue, and pinch the crimp end closed (**e**). Repeat on the other end of the cord.
3. Repeat Step 2 on the other cord.
4. Use a jump ring to attach one end of each cord length to the clasp (**f**). String three spacers over both cords. (**g**).
5. Use a jump ring to attach the other end of each cord length to the S clasp.

To wear the bracelet, double up and hook the S clasp into the bezel.

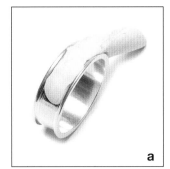
a

b

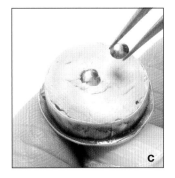
c

d

e

f

g

tip Use the same metals within a piece like this. For example, sterling pieces deserve sterling findings, and ornate pieces deserve ornate findings. These bezel clasps were designed by Susan Lenart Kazmer. Her findings have an industrial feel that I like, so I wanted to use findings that complemented the bezel's style.

Under Lock and Key Chain

What better way to secure a chunky chain than to lock it up? Doubling as a clasp, this lock isn't only functional, it's also a great accent.

Crystals
variety of crystals, all Art. 2028
SS10 Black Diamond
SS8 Crystal Moonlight
SS6 Black Diamond
SS6 Jet
SS3 Crystal

Materials
20- or 24-in. (51–61cm) 8mm silver cable chain
lock clasp (Rio Grande, riogrande.com)
two-part epoxy glue (30 min.)

Tools:
flush cutters
syringe
tweezers
toothpick

a

b

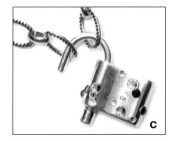

c

tip Double or triple the chain around your wrist for a bracelet version. Simply lock the chain ends and you're good to go.

Decorate the clasp
1. On a flat surface, plan a crystal pattern pretty side up. I used a monochromatic color palette of different sizes and made a random design.
2. Mix epoxy (Basics) and apply the glue to the lock with a syringe (**a**), adding crystals as you go (**b**). Repeat around the lock.
3. Set aside until completely dry (overnight is best).

Finish the necklace
4. Cut the chain to your desired length and clasp the lock onto both ends (**c**).

Fibers

Soft and elegant fabric and **fibers** are a refreshing **balance** for hard-edged crystals. Irresistible dyed silks, fun and **funky felts**, supple **leather**, and soft **ribbon** are so tempting! Color and **texture** choices abound. Have fun mixing your materials for an **unexpected** presentation.

Velvet Ribbon Bracelet

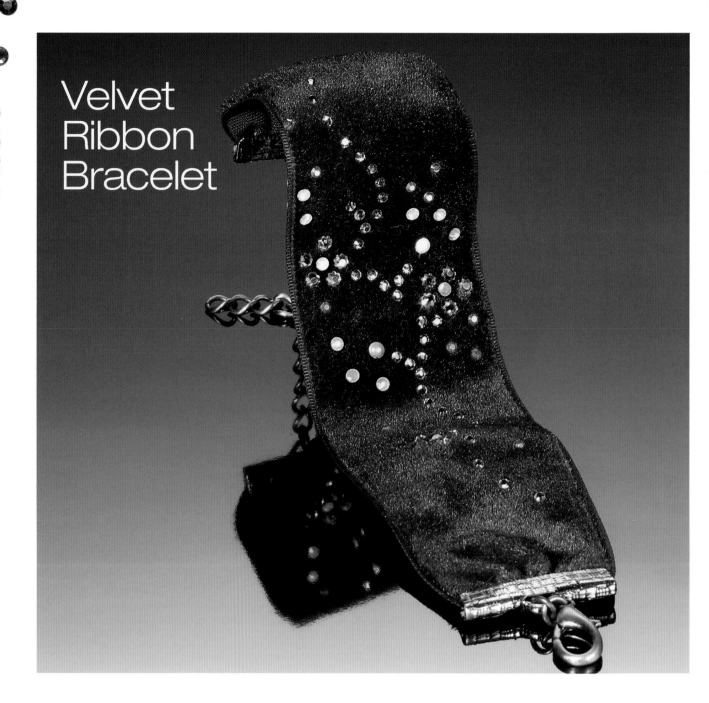

Lush velvet is a luxe backdrop for a crystal flower motif. What could be simpler? All you need is an iron and a few minutes of your time.

Crystals
bracelet
iron-on hot-fix transfer
earrings
hot-fix Art. 2028 crystals

Materials
bracelet
- 7 in. (18cm) 2-in. (5cm) wide velvet ribbon
- 2 1½ in. (3.8cm) aged end bars
- 4 in. (10cm) brass cable chain
- 12mm brass lobster clasp
- 2 5mm brass jump rings
- two-part epoxy glue (30 min.)

earrings
5 in. (13cm) ribbon
2 1-in. (2.5cm) aged end bars
pair of earring wires

Tools (both projects)
sewing needle and thread
parchment paper
iron
2 pairs chainnose pliers

Embellish the ribbon with crystals

1. Heat iron to 320°.

2. Lay the ribbon on a flat, heat-resistant surface.

3. Peel the backing from the transfer. Lay the transfer on the surface with the adhesive side against the top (right) side of the ribbon. Iron the clear plastic until the crystals are adhered to the ribbon (about 20 to 30 seconds) (**a**). Let the ribbon and transfer cool completely and then gently remove the clear plastic. If a stone remains on the plastic, place it back on the ribbon and iron again.

Make the bracelet

4. With a threaded needle, stitch the end of the ribbon and pull the thread to gather it. Tie off and trim extra thread. Repeat on the other end (**b**).

5. Open the metal ribbon end and dab the inside with glue. Position the gathered ribbon end. Pinch with chain-nose pliers to secure (**c**). Repeat on the other end.

Finish the bracelet

6. Attach chain to the bracelet end loop with a jump ring (**d**).

7. Repeat on the other side, substituting a clasp for the chain.

Earrings

1. With a hot-fix applicator wand (see p. 10—11), add a crystal design to a 2¼-in. long ribbon. Begin at the center, and work your way to one end.

2. Fold the ribbon in half and sew as you did in Step 4.

3. Add a metal ribbon end, as you did in Step 5.

4. Complete the earrings by opening the loop of an earring wire and attach the ribbon form. Close the loop. Make a second earring to match the first.

a

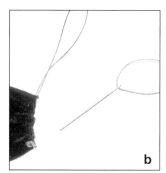
b

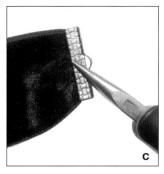
c

d

tip Place a piece of parchment paper behind the ribbon while adding crystals with the hot-fix tool. The parchment will prevent the project from adhering to your work surface if the adhesive seeps through.

tip To help the transfer adhere to your ribbon, iron the ribbon first. Heating fabric or ribbon before applying a transfer helps activate the adhesive, which holds the transfer in place and creates a better bond.

Sands of Time

Sand-colored silk strands sprinkled with crystals surround a beautiful glass shell pendant, evoking memories of sun-drenched days on the beach.

Crystals (hot-fix Art. 2028)
24 SS12 Lt. Colorado Topaz
24 SS8 Crystal Golden Shadow
24 SS6 Lt. Amethyst
24 SS10 Smoked Topaz
24 SS16 Lt. Grey Opal
24 SS16 Crystal AB

Materials
38mm sea shell glass pendant (Sonoran Beads, sonoranbeads.com)
2 glass end caps (Sonoran Beads)

42 x ¾-in. (107 x 1.9cm) silk ribbons, one each of three colors: taupe, sand, and sea foam (Silk Painting is Fun, Silkpaintingisfun.com)
42 in. (107cm) 2mm silk string, robin's egg (Silk Painting is Fun)
18-in. (46cm) 22-gauge silver wire
2 5mm silver jump rings
2 2½-in. (6.4cm) silver eye pins
toggle clasp

Tools
hot-fix tool
chainnose pliers
roundnose pliers
flush cutters

Make the necklace

1. Fold a 4-in. (10cm) length of wire in half. Carefully catch a ribbon and the string in the fold, and use the wire to guide the ribbons through the focal bead (**a**). Center the bead on the ribbons.

2. Place a ribbon on a heat-resistant flat surface. Heat the hot-fix tool and adhere a random pattern of crystals to the ribbon (**b**) (see p. 10–11). Repeat with the remaining ribbons.

3. Once you are happy with the design, turn the ribbons over and repeat the same pattern on the reverse side. Place crystals directly over those on the first side.

Finish the necklace

4. Place the focal-bead strand and the two crystal-coated ribbons on the work surface.

5. On each side of the pendant, tie an overhand knot with two of the four ribbons approximately 2½ in. (6.4cm) from the center (**c**). Tie another overhand knot on each side 1½ in. (3.8cm) from the last knot using a different combination of ribbons. Repeat once more, if desired.

6. Determine the length of your necklace. Cut a 4-in. (10cm) length of 20-gauge wire. Make a wrapped loop (Basics) on one end. Fold the ribbon ends over and lay the loop on top of the ribbons. Wrap the wire stem around all the ribbon (**d**). Trim excess wire and ribbon.

7. Open the loop of a 2½ in. eye pin (Basics). Attach it to the wrapped loop. String a glass end cap (**e**). Make a loop above the end cap. Repeat on the other side. Attach a toggle clasp half to each loop (**f**).

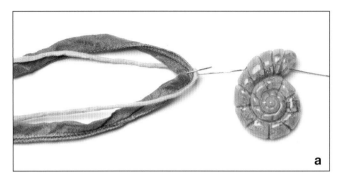

a

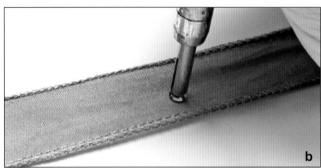

b

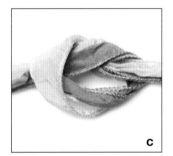

c

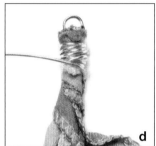

d

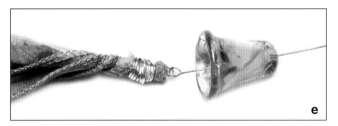

e

f

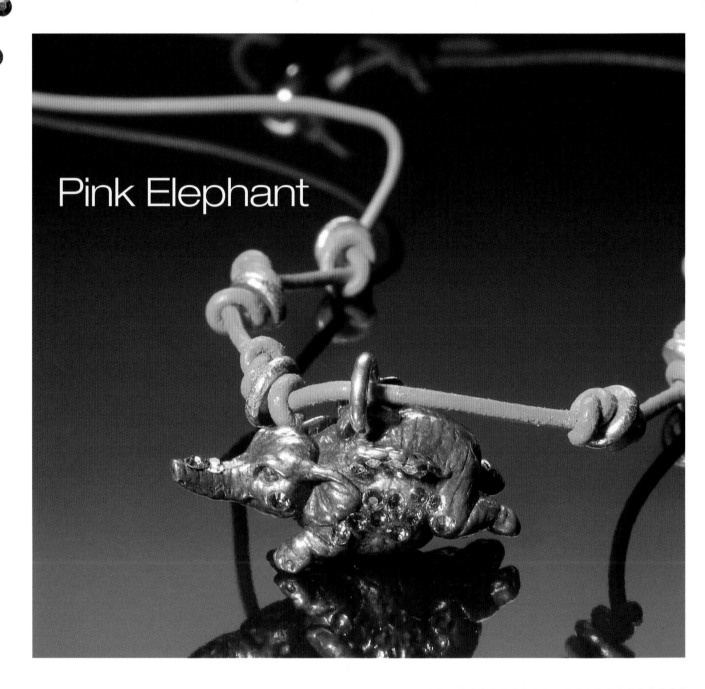

Pink Elephant

Crystals bring flash and personality to a casual pewter charm from Green Girl Studios; metal accent beads tie the look together.

Flying Elephant
10 SS3 Art. 2028 Crystal
25 SS6 Art. 2028 Lt. Amethyst
flying elephant pendant
   (Green Girl Studios,
   greengirlstudios.com)
6–8 10mm silver heishi beads
large silver bead for clasp
30 in. (76cm) cord
two-part epoxy glue (30 min.)

Bumble Friend
14 SS3 Art. 2028 Crystal
27 SS5 Art. 2028 Citrine

13 3mm Art. 2415, Jet Metallic
   Silver
bumble friend pendant (Green
   Girl Studios)
6–8 6mm antiqued brass
   heishi beads
large brass bead for clasp
54 in. (1.4m) 4-ply waxed linen
   cord, black
two-part epoxy glue (30 min.)

Tools (both projects)
tweezers or wax stick
toothpick or syringe
cutters

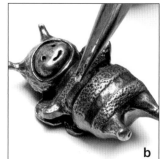

Prepare charms for both necklaces

Mix epoxy (Basics). Apply glue with either a toothpick or syringe where you'd like to add crystals. Let glue set for a few minutes, then add crystals with tweezers or wax stick (**a**, **b**).

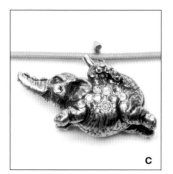

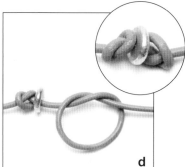

Make the elephant necklace

1. Center the pendant on the cord (**c**).
2. On each side, tie an overhand knot, string a heishi, and tie another overhand knot (**d**). Repeat twice, spacing the beads as desired.
3. On one end, tie a knot, string a large silver bead, and tie a knot flush to the other side of the bead (**e**). On the other end, tie a loop large enough to go over the end bead but snug enough to secure the necklace.

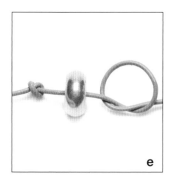

Make the bumble friend necklace

Follow Steps 1–3 of the elephant necklace, substituting two strands of waxed linen for the cord and antiqued brass beads for the silver (**f**).

Can't get the cord through your bead? Cut the end on a slight angle for easier stringing.

Garden Party

Energize your summer wardrobe with a bouquet of flowers and hammered gold rings—you'll feel the warm rays of the sun even on a cloudy day!

Crystals
Variety of sizes Art. 2028 crystals (use colors that accent or match your felt flowers and beads)

Materials
11 2cm felt balls, spectrum colors (Ornamentea, ornamentea.com)
2 felt flowers, spectrum colors (Ornamentea)
8 17mm VeeO Vogue II Ring Textured (Via Murano, viamurano.com)

4 21mm VeeO Vogue II Ring Textured (Via Murano)
4 27mm VeeO Vogue II Ring Textured (Via Murano)
2 44mm VeeO Vogue II Ring Textured (Via Murano)
22 9mm gold-filled jump rings
20 2-in. (5cm) gold-filled head pins
gold-tone fancy flowers (Decorative Details/Nunn Design nunndesign.com)
18 in. (46cm) 3mm gold-filled oval curb chain
two-part epoxy glue (30 min.)

Tools
hot-fix tool
rotary tool with ⅜- or ⅝-in. (1/1.6cm) bit
2 pairs chainnose pliers
roundnose pliers
flush cutters

tip **Brads** originally designed for scrapbooking add an unexpected touch.

Make flowers

1. Heat the hot-fix tool (see p. 10–11).

2. Drill through the center of felt flowers and balls (**a**) and immediately string on a 2½ in. (6.4cm) head pin (**b**). (Drilling makes it easier for the head pin to go through the felt. Stringing immediately helps you remember where the hole is.) Make two flowers.

3. Mix epoxy (Basics). Add crystals to the center of each flower (**c**).

4. Put a dab of glue at the head of a 2½-in. head pin, string a felt ball (**d**), and make a wrapped loop (Basics). Make six. Use the hot-fix tool to add crystals to three and leave three plain.

5. Mix epoxy (Basics). Use a toothpick to apply glue to the center of a metal brad flower. Let glue set for a few minutes and then add a crystal to the center (**e**). Make two.

6. On a 2½-in. head pin, put a dab of glue at the base, string a crystal-embellished felt ball and one or two hanging brads (**f**), and make a wrapped loop (Basics) above the beads. Make three. With the hot-fix tool, add crystals, varying the amount on each. (This will make your design more interesting.)

7. On a 2½-in. head pin, string a felt ball, metal flower, and a hanging brad, and make a wrapped loop. Use the hot-fix tool to add crystals.

Make the necklace

8. Place rings as shown and connect with jump rings (Basics) to create segments A, B, and C. Close the jump rings as you go (**g**).

9. Cut four 1½-in. (3.8cm) lengths of chain. Use a jump ring to link a chain end to each side of segments B and C from step 8. Close the jump rings.

10. Use a jump ring to connect both ends of chain from B to one end of segment A. Repeat to attach segment C to the other side of segment A (**h**).

11. Open a jump ring and attach 5 in. (13cm) of chain to the center ring on one end of the necklace. Close the jump ring. Open a jump ring and link three plain felt balls and the end of the chain (**i**). Close the jump ring.

12. Cut a 3-in. (7.6cm) chain segment. Open a jump ring and link one end of chain to the center ring of the other end of the necklace. Close the jump ring. Open a jump ring and attach the other end of chain to the remaining ring. Close the jump ring (**j**).

13. Spread out the necklace and the remaining felt pieces. Open two jump rings and working from the center, place the two felt flowers. Close the jump rings. Open 10 jump rings, and continue adding the felt pieces in a pleasing design. Close the jump rings as you go.

Feel free to make adjustments and move felt pieces around until you're happy with the look.

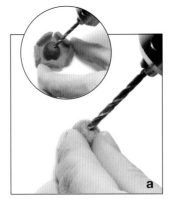

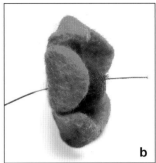

a

b

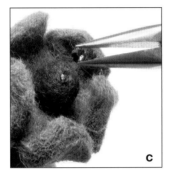

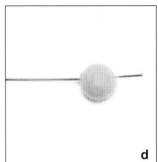

c

d

e

f

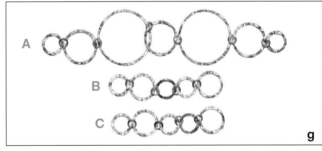

A

B

C

g

h

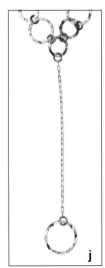

j

i

"Wow! I Coulda Had a Tagua!"

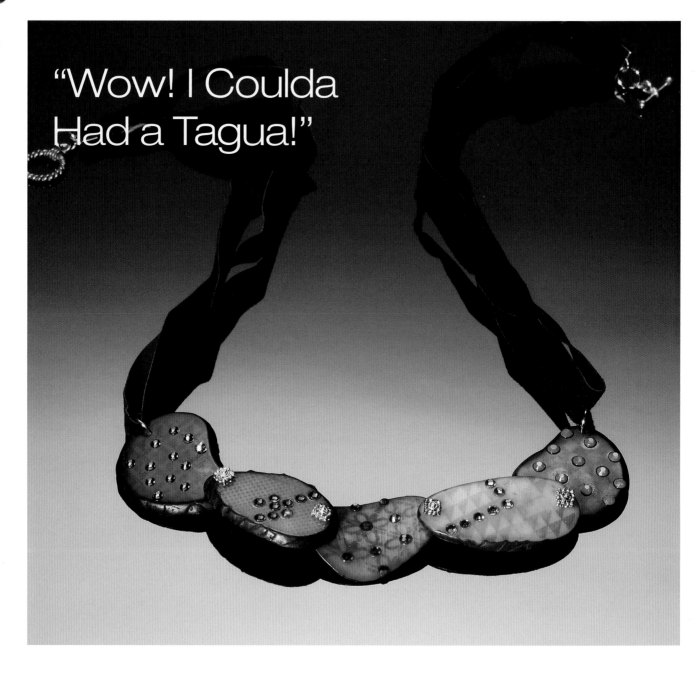

Commonly referred to as "vegetable ivory," nuts from the tagua palm tree are carved into beads, buttons, and decorative objects. These colorful slices have been dyed and are the perfect backdrop for vibrant crystals.

Crystals (all SS10 Art. 2028)
color A Tanzanite
color B Olivine
color C Topaz
color D Fuchsia
color E Capri Blue

Materials
5 tagua slices, variety of colors (On the Surface, onsurface.com)
4 decorative silver head pins
36 in. (.9m) black suede ribbon cut in half
2 ribbon ends to fit suede
4 8mm jump rings
toggle clasp
rubber stamps in five patterns
permanent ink
two-part epoxy glue (30 min.)

Tools
rotary tool with ⅜-in. (1cm) bit
tweezers
toothpick
chainnose pliers
roundnose pliers
flush cutters

Prepare tagua nut slices

1. Drill holes in opposite sides of a tagua slice (**a**).

2. Ink rubber stamp with permanent dye and stamp the tagua slice. Repeat, using a different stamp on each slice (**b**). Set aside to dry.

3. Overlap two slices and string a head pin through both holes (**c**).

4. Trim the end of the head pin to ⅜ in. (1cm) and make a plain loop (Basics). Bend the loop flat against the back of the slice (**d**).

5. Repeat to connect the remaining slices.

Add crystals

6. Mix epoxy (Basics). Use a toothpick or a syringe to apply glue to the nut. Add crystals. Repeat, using different crystal colors on each slice (**e**).

7. Set aside to dry.

Finish necklace

8. Open a jump ring (Basics) and attach to one end of the row of slices. Repeat on the other end.

9. On one end, string a ribbon through the jump ring (**f**) and close the jump ring. Center the ribbon.

10. Bring the ends together. Use chainnose pliers to pinch the ribbon end over both ends (**g**). (I added a dab of glue.)

11. Repeat Steps 9–10 on the other end.

12. Open a jump ring and attach half of the toggle clasp (**h**). Close the jump ring. Repeat on the other end with the remaining clasp half.

fact Did you know that export of the tagua nut employs nearly 35,000 native workers? Found in the rainforests of Ecuador, Colombia, and Peru, the tagua nut has been made into beads since the 19th century. The importance of the tagua nut to the local economies is a strong incentive to maintain trees and ultimately stabilize the rain forest.

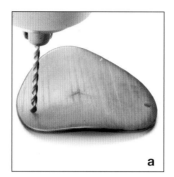

a

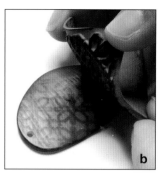

b

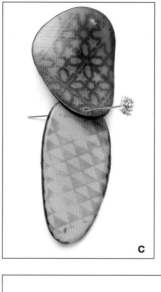

c

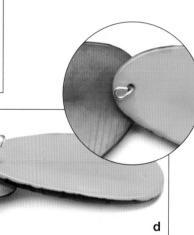

d

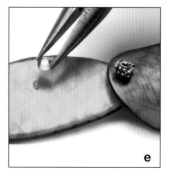

e

f

g

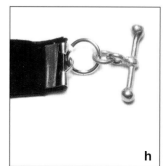

h

Wild One

Let your wild side shine with a leopard-print ribbon and a sprinkling of crystals—all caged in a bold, gold chain.

Crystals (all hot-fix Art. 2028)
SS10 Smoked Topaz
SS8 Crystal Golden Shadow
SS8 Jet Nut
SS10 Smoked Topaz
SS10 Black Diamond

Materials
24 in. (61cm) large-link gold-finish chain
36 in. (.9m) 1½-in. (3.8cm) wide ribbon
2 3-in. (7.6cm) gold-finish head pins or 6 in. (15cm) length gold wire

toggle clasp
6–8 10mm jump rings
parchment paper

Tools
hot fix applicator
roundnose pliers
2 pairs of chainnose pliers

Embellish the ribbon with crystals

1. Heat the hot-fix tool.

2. Place ribbon on a heat-resistant surface covered with parchment paper.

3. Use the hot-fix tool to add a random pattern of crystals (Basics).

4. Once you are happy with the design, let the ribbon cool completely before finishing the necklace.

Finish the necklace

5. Cut the chain to desired finished length of necklace, allowing 1 in. (2.5cm) for the clasp.

6. Fold the ribbon in half and weave it through the chain links (**a, b**), gently easing the fixed crystals through the links.

7. On one end, fold the edge of the ribbon over the last link of chain.

8. Trim the end from a head pin or a use a 3-in. (7.6cm) piece of wire and make a loop on one end (Basics).

9. Add the ribbon to the loop. Hold the loop with chainnose pliers and start to pull the wire around the folded ribbon with a second pair of chainnose pliers (**c**). Complete the wraps, trapping the ribbon end in the wire. Trim the excess wire and ribbon. Repeat on the other side.

10. Open three jump rings (Basics). Connect one ring to one end link of chain. Connect a second ring to the first. Connect a third jump ring to one half of the toggle clasp and the previous jump ring (**d**). Repeat on the other end, substituting the other clasp half. Adjust the fit by adding or removing jump rings.

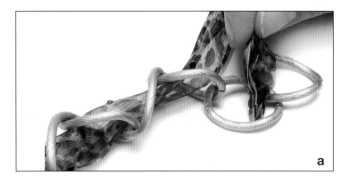

a

b

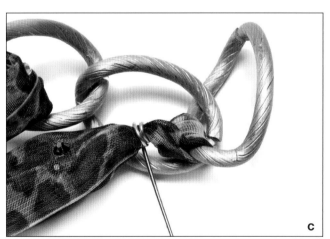

c

d

Eye Candy

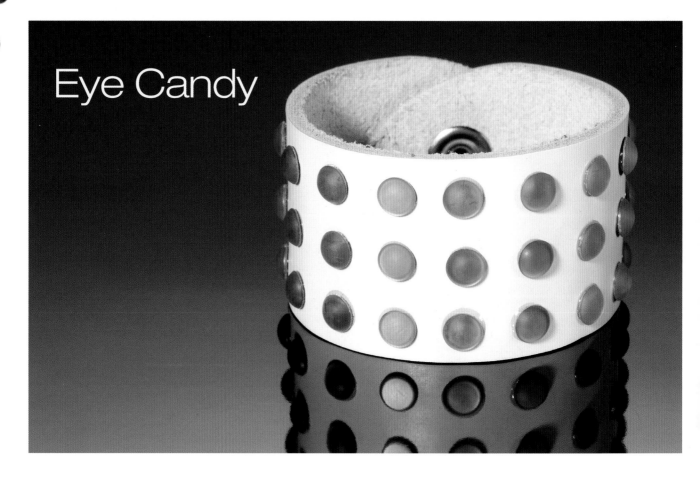

Copy the look of penny candy buttons with unfaceted crystals in candy colors! These sugary sweeties are a candy-store classic; your grown-up version will be a flashback favorite.

Crystals (all crystals are SS16 Art. 2080)
24 Light Rose
24 Sapphire
24 Topaz

Materials
leather bracelet cuff
(Sole Survivor,
solesurvivorleather.com)

two-part epoxy (30 min.)
carbon transfer paper

Tools
syringe
tweezers
toothpick

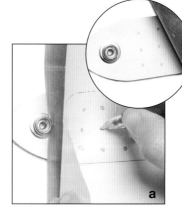

a

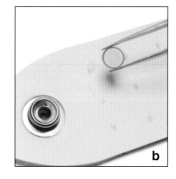

b

enlarge to 200%

1. Use carbon paper to transfer pattern to leather cuff (**a**).
2. Mix epoxy (Basics). Apply glue with either a toothpick or syringe to the front of the cuff.
3. Let glue set for a few minutes and then add the crystals (**b**). To mimic the candy dot pattern, I set four rows of three crystals in three colors.

Polymer clay is a **simple substance** that can result in **gallery**-worthy pieces of art and jewelry. Crystals are an excellent **embellishment** for polymer clay because they withstand the baking temperature without harm. Enjoy the **possibilities** open to you with this versatile medium, and push the limits!

Polymer Clay

Honeycomb

Crystals
36 SS16 Art. 2028 hot fix,
    Cathedral Topaz AB

Materials
polymer clay, black
32 x 30mm copper oval
    screen ring (Ornamentea,
    ornamentea.com)
silver bee charm (Blue Mud,
    bluemud.com)
liver of sulfur
sandpaper
two-part epoxy glue (30 min.)

Tools
small container
rolling pin
craft knife
tweezers
flush cutters

Try this polymer-enhanced ring on for size. Its subtle colors befit the golden hues of a true honeycomb. Fit for a queen (bee), this jeweled creation will have you reigning with style!

tip Hard-boiled eggs are a good substitute for liver of sulfur. Simply hang the charm in a container filled with a chopped egg and cover until it's the color you like; then remove the charm and rinse. The gases from the cooked egg will oxidize the silver.

Prepare the ring

1. Take the mesh dome off the ring base.

2. Knead and roll out the polymer clay. Press the mesh dome lightly into the rolled clay (**a**).

3. Cut around the impression with a craft knife (**b**).

4. Cover the mesh dome with the cut clay (**c**). Form and shape until the clay is smooth and even.

5. Attach the covered mesh dome to the ring base (**d**). With chainnose pliers, gently bend the prongs to secure.

Add crystals

6. Row 1: Add three crystals to the ring form (**e**). With tweezers, place and gently push the crystals into the clay to create a raised bezel around them.

7. Row 2: Add four crystals offset from the crystals in the first row, mimicking a honeycomb pattern. Allow black clay to show through, adding to the honeycomb effect (**f**). Row 3: Add five crystals, offset from row 2. Row 4: Add six crystals, offset from row 3. Rows 6–9: add five, six, four, and three crystals, respectively.

8. Place the ring in an oven-safe dish of uncooked rice so the ring will be upright while baking. Follow the polymer clay manufacturer's directions to bake (usually 275°, 15 minutes for each ¼-in./6mm thickness). Clay should be hard but still a little flexible. The adhesive on the back of the crystals will melt during baking and glue the crystal to the clay. No additional gluing is necessary unless a stone happens to come loose. Cool completely.

Add the bee charm

9. Dilute a small chunk of liver of sulfur in a small container filled with warm water. With tweezers, dip the silver charm into the liquid (**g**). Remove when the desired effect is reached. Rinse with water and dry.

10. With flush cutters, trim the charm loop (**h**).

11. Gently sand the charm with sandpaper to reveal some of the silver color (**i**).

12. Mix epoxy (Basics). Using toothpick, apply glue to the back of the charm. Let the glue set for a minute or two. Adhere the charm to the front of the ring (**j**). Stabilize the ring in a container of rice until the glue is completely dry.

tip

You can use regular flat-back crystals since the clay will make a bezel around the stone, but hot-fix crystals add extra strength.

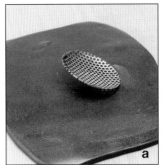

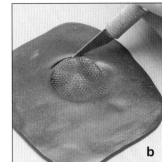

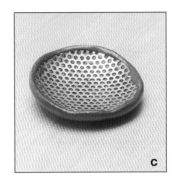

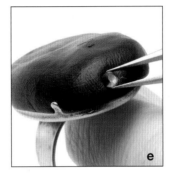

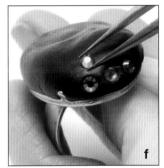

Charmed

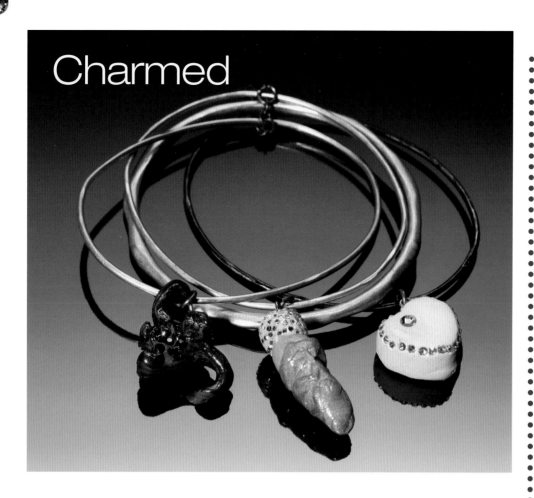

Create charms that have all the elegance of enameled and pavé jewelry seen on Fifth Avenue. Embellish ready-made bangles or cuffs and turn these charms into a full-blown bracelet.

Ice Cream Cone
Crystals
SS3 Art. 2028 hot fix, Crystal
Clay
beige
pink
off-white

Heart
Crystals
SS5 Art. 2028 hot fix, Crystal AB
Clay
white
pink

Monkey
Crystals
SS8 Art. 2028 hot fix, Jet
Clay
white
black

Materials
polymer glaze (Translucent
    Liquid Sculpey)
embossing powder
2 eye pins
3 3mm jump rings
3 or 4 thin bangles
3 in. (7.6cm) 3mm brass
    cable chain
brass snap clasp
bangle bracelets
plastic monkey
candy heart

Tools
syringe
tweezers
2 pairs of chainnose pliers
small rolling pin
rubber texture stamp
craft knife

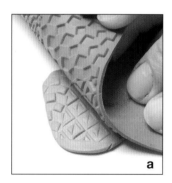

a

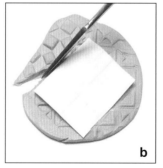

b

c

d

Make polymer charms:
Ice cream cone
1. Knead and roll out beige polymer clay. Texture the clay with the rubber stamp (**a**). Gently lift stamp.
2. Using a craft knife, cut a ¾-in. x ½-in. (1.9 x 1.3cm) rectangle from the textured clay (**b**).
3. Roll a pea-sized ball of white clay. Repeat with pink. Stack the two balls of clay as if you were making an ice cream cone. Wrap the "cone" around the stacked clay balls. Trim a head pin to ½ in. Make a plain loop (Basics)

at the end and push the other end into the top of the ice cream cone charm (**c**).

4. Lightly rub embossing powder over the raised edges of the textured cone (**d**).

Heart

1. Using white polymer clay and a candy heart, make a mold (Basics, p. 12). Follow the polymer clay manufacturer's directions to bake. (Usually 275°, 15 minutes for each ¼-in./6mm thickness.) Clay should be hard but still a little flexible. Cool completely.

2. Knead the pink polymer clay. Push kneaded clay into the mold (**e**). Gently lift out of mold. (Tip: Put the mold and clay in the freezer for a few minutes. This makes the clay harder, and it will come out more easily without stretching or distorting.)

3. Trim an eye pin to ½ in. With chainnose pliers, slightly bend the end (**f**). Push into the top of the charm (**g**).

4. Using a craft knife, trim excess clay (**h**).

Monkey

1. As you did with the candy heart, make a mold with a plastic monkey. Use black clay and follow Step 2 of the heart to make a polymer monkey. Trim any excess clay.

2. Embed a 3mm jump ring in the back of the casting (**i**). Cover with a bit of polymer clay to secure (**j**).

Add crystals

1. With tweezers, gently push a crystal into the clay (**k**) to create a natural raised bezel around the crystal. Continue as desired.

2. Place decorated charm (or charms) in an oven-safe dish of uncooked rice or tin foil mold to keep upright while baking.

3. Bake according to the polymer clay manufacturer's directions (usually 275°, 15 minutes for each ¼-in./6mm thickness of clay). Clay should be hard but still a little flexible. The adhesive on the back of the crystal will melt during the baking time and glue the crystal to the clay. No additional gluing is necessary unless a stone comes loose. Cool completely.

Finish charms

1. Brush on a light coat of polymer glaze (Translucent Liquid Sculpey) (**l**), allowing time to dry between coats. Add more coats for an even glossier look.

Make the charm bracelet

1. Cut a 1½- or 2-in. chain length (depending on how thick your bangles are). Open a jump ring (Basics) and connect half the snap clasp to one end link of chain (**m**). Repeat on the other end of the chain to add the other part of the clasp. Clasp the chain around the bangles (**n**).

2. Open a jump ring and attach one charm to one bangle (**o**). Repeat, adding a new charm onto a new bangle. Repeat with the last charm.

e

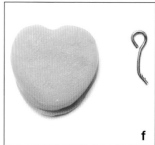

f

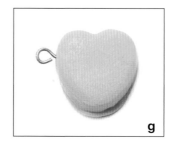

g

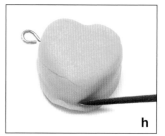

h

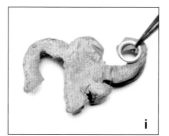

i

j

k

l

m

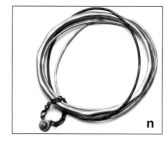

n

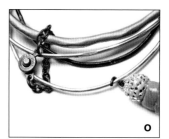

o

Gem of a Specimen

Let the light shine on delicate poppy petals, made from polymer clay. Flourishing crystals play up the bright orange-red hues of this stunning flower.

Crystals (all Art. 2028 hot fix in assorted sizes and colors)
SS8 Light Siam
SS8 Topaz
SS8 Hyacinth
SS10 Aquamarine Cosmo Jet

Material
poppy mold
polymer clay: black, red, orange, and warm yellow
pin back

Tools
craft knife
acrylic roller
needle tool
tweezers
toothpick
parchment paper
baking sheet

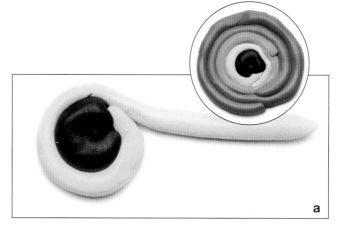

Make the poppy

1. Knead each polymer clay color separately. Roll each color into a snake roll. Spiral the black snake roll into a coil the size of your poppy's center. Coil the yellow roll around the outside edge of black spiral once (**a** with inset); trim excess. Repeat with the orange roll. Finish with the red roll. Note: The finished shape should be about the size of the interior of the mold.

2. Close the clay seams with your fingers (**b**).

3. Gently roll over shape with an acrylic roller to combine all the coil shapes (**c**).

4. Using a needle tool, draw veins in flower from center out (**d**), dragging the different colors throughout the flower as you work.

5. With your fingers, even out the clay

6. Press the clay firmly into the mold (**e**).

7. Press the pin back in place and secure with scrap clay (**f**).

8. Refrigerate or freeze for a few minutes. This step hardens the clay and makes it easier to remove it from the mold without pulling or distorting the casting. Remove the clay from the mold and let it return to room temperature.

Add crystals

9. Add crystals to the cast flower. Play up the texture and colors of petals (**g**).

Finish the pin

10. Bake the pin in a pan lined with parchment paper with the pin back side up.

11. Follow the polymer clay manufacturer's directions to bake (usually 275°, 15 minutes for each ¼-in./6mm thickness). Clay should be hard but still a little flexible. The adhesive on the back of the crystals will melt during the baking time and glue the crystal to the clay. No additional gluing is necessary unless a stone happens to come loose. Cool completely.

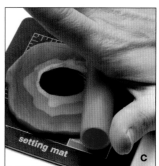

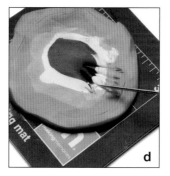

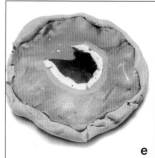

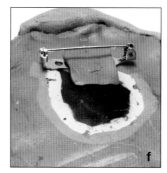

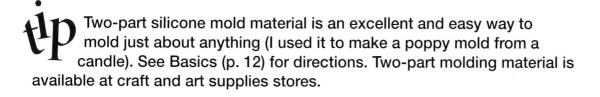

tip Two-part silicone mold material is an excellent and easy way to mold just about anything (I used it to make a poppy mold from a candle). See Basics (p. 12) for directions. Two-part molding material is available at craft and art supplies stores.

Stamp Out

Made from stamped polymer clay panels, this bangle is enhanced with crystals and Pearl Ex powders for an unexpected twist.

Crystals
variety of colors and sizes of hot-fix crystals (I used SS6, Lt Amethyst; SS10, Amethyst; and SS6, Purple Velvet.)

Materials
polymer clay (I used beige and gray)
8 16mm brass jump rings (Vintaj Natural Brass Co., Vintaj.com)
Pearl Ex embossing powder

rubber stamps in a variety of patterns
two-part epoxy glue (30 min.)

Tools
small rolling pin
polymer cutting blade
craft knife
needle tool
tweezers
cylindrical object, such as an empty paper towel tube

Make the bracelet segments

1. Knead and roll out polymer clay. Texture the clay with a rubber stamp (**a**). Gently lift stamp.

2. Using a polymer cutting blade, cut clay to 2 x 2 in. (5 x 5cm) (**b**).

3. With a needle tool, make a hole about ¼ in. (6mm) from each corner (**c**).

4. Lightly dust the raised areas with Pearl Ex powder (**d**).

5. Repeat to make a total of four squares. (I used two different colors of clay.)

Add crystals

6. Plan your design on a flat work surface.

7. With tweezers, gently push crystals into the clay (**e**) to create a raised bezel around the crystals.

8. After placing all the crystals, lay the squares over a cylinder, supporting with aluminum foil if necessary (**f**). Place on an oven-safe tray. Follow the polymer clay manufacturer's directions to bake (usually 275°, 15 minutes for each ¼-in./6mm thickness). Clay should be hard but still a little flexible. The adhesive on the back of the crystals will melt during the baking time, gluing the crystals to the clay. No additional gluing is necessary unless a stone happens to come loose. Cool completely.

Finish the bangle

9. Open eight jump rings (Basics). Connect the panels with jump rings (**g**). Close the jump rings as you work.

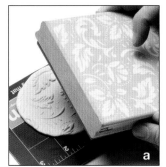

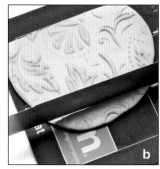

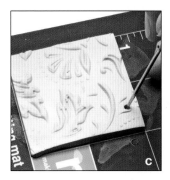

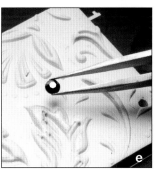

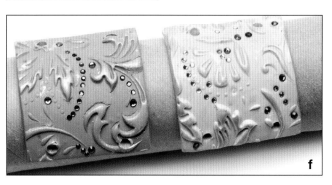

Use the same technique to make textured buttons and a custom button-and-loop closure for a simple bracelet.

Fused Two-gether

The secret to these elegant earrings is hidden beneath the clay. The filigree form provides a lightweight base, making them comfortable to wear.

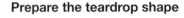

Crystals (all Art. 2028 hot fix)
SS12 Light Grey Opal
SS10 White Opal
SS10 Light Amethyst
SS8 Light Amethyst
SS5 Citrine
SS5 Crystal AB
SS3 Crystal

Materials
2 brass ear wires (Vintaj Natural
  Brass Co., vintaj.com)

2 filigree teardrop bead forms
  (Vintaj Natural Brass Co.)
polymer clay, beige

Tools
craft knife
syringe
tweezers
2 pairs chainnose pliers
roundnose pliers

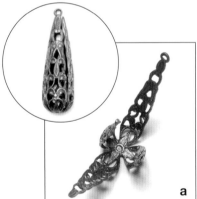

a

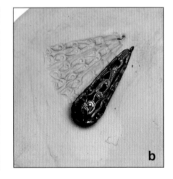

b

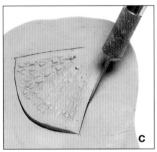

c

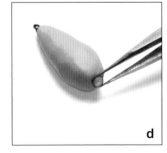

d

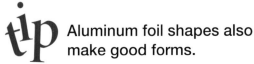

tip Aluminum foil shapes also make good forms.

Prepare the teardrop shape

1. Because the filigree form comes flat and needs to be shaped before starting, use chainnose pliers to bend the edges of the form into a teardrop shape (**a**).

2. Knead and roll out the polymer clay. Roll the teardrop across the clay, pressing lightly (**b**).

3. Use a craft knife to cut out the impression (**c**). Form and shape the cut clay onto the teardrop until smooth and even.

Add crystals

4. Place one crystal in the center of the bottom of the teardrop (**d**).

5. Add a row at a time, working from bottom to top and randomly placing different sizes and colors of crystals until the shape is covered. (Use smaller crystals to fill in and be sure some clay shows through.) Repeat to make a second teardrop.

6. Support the teardrops in an oven-safe dish of uncooked rice or a foil mold so they are upright while baking. Follow the polymer clay manufacturer's directions to bake (usually 275°, 15 minutes for each ¼-in. (6mm) thickness). Clay should be hard but still a little flexible. The adhesive on the back of the crystals will melt during the baking time and glue the crystal to the clay. No additional gluing is necessary unless a stone happens to come loose. Cool completely.

Finish the earrings

7. Open the loop of an earring wire (Basics p. 13) and attach the filigree form. Close the loop. Repeat with the second earring.

Resin

Technically, resin is a copal or mastic material that consists of amorphous mixtures of carboxylic acids obtained directly from certain plants as exudations or prepared by polymerization of simple molecules and used in the making of varnishes and plastics. Phew! Resin is a lot more fun to play with than this definition leads you to believe. In this chapter, you'll work with some resin forms, and you'll also learn how to mix your own.

Bezel, Bezel

Create your own gems by filling silver settings with patterned paper and tiny crystals. Make it permanent with quick-setting resin.

This version uses slide bezels and a watch band for a completely different look.

Crystals
Art. 2006 crystals in a variety of sizes, shapes, and colors

Materials
both projects
epoxy resin kit
two-part epoxy glue (30 min.)

bracelet
5 small deep-link circle bezels
patterned paper in five patterns
7 8mm jump rings
2 5mm jump rings
toggle clasp

necklace
large bail mount circle bezel
steel cable necklace form with clasp
patterned paper

Tools
tweezers
toothpick
syringe (optional)
wooden stick
2 pairs chainnose pliers

supply note: bezels are from Patera, nunndesigns.com; cable necklace is from Rings & Things, rings-things.com

Prepare the paper
1. Cut assorted papers into shapes to fit each bezel.
2. Mix epoxy (Basics). Use a toothpick or a syringe to apply the glue where you'd like the crystals. Let the glue set for a few minutes, and then add crystals with tweezers or wax stick.
3. Let the glue dry completely (overnight is best).

Fill the bezels
4. Following the manufacturer's directions, mix equal parts of resin and hardener (Basics, p. 12). Mix completely.
5. Stabilize the bezel in a container of rice. Fill halfway with mixed resin (**a**).
6. Holding the paper with tweezers, slide paper into the resin-filled bezel (**b**).
7. Push the paper to the bottom of the bezel with a toothpick (**c**).
8. Add more resin to fill the bezel (**d**).
9. Repeat Steps 5–8 to complete all of the bezels. Let the resin harden completely. (According to the manufacturer's instructions, it usually takes 24 hours. After the resin has hardened, it will take a few days for the resin to cure completely. Be careful when handling.)

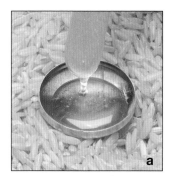
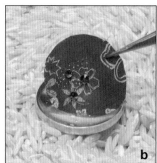

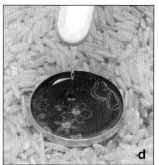

tip Sliding the paper into the resin and pushing down with a toothpick helps eliminate air bubbles that can be trapped under the paper and ultimately harden in the resin.

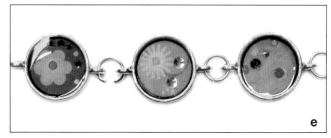

Make the bracelet
1. Open an 8mm jump ring (Basics). Link two bezels (**e**) and close the jump ring. Continue to add bezels with jump rings until all five are linked together.
2. On one end, attach an 8mm jump ring, a 5mm jump ring, and an 8mm jump ring. Open the 8mm ring and attach the toggle bar (**f**). Close the jump ring.
3. On the other end, attach an 8mm jump ring. Open a 5mm jump ring, link the last 8mm ring and the toggle loop, and close the jump ring (**g**). Add or remove jump rings to adjust the fit.

Make the necklace
1. Follow Steps 1–3 of "Prepare the paper" and 4–8 of "Fill the bezels" to make a pendant (**h**).
2. String the pendant on the cable necklace (**i**).

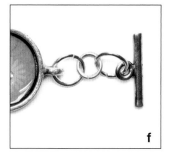

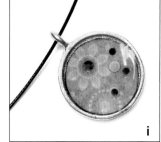

Egg-cellent Locket

Set your fabulous photos in a glass-like finish. Did Mr. Bunny hide the crystals inside?

Crystals (all Art. 2028)
8 SS5 Crystal AB
9 SS8 Fuchsia
5 SS12 Crystal AB
17 SS10 Aquamarine
5 SS6 Black Citrine

Materials
brass egg locket (Ornamentea, ornamentea.com)
two photographs
3 5mm brass jump rings
24 in. (61cm) 6mm brass oval chain (Vintaj Natural Brass Co., vintaj.com)

8 x 13mm antique brass spring clasp (Vintaj Natural Brass Co.)
Judi-Kins Amazing Glaze embossing powder
two-part epoxy glue (5 min.)

Tools
craft stick
2 pairs of chainnose pliers
toothpicks
tweezers or wax stick

Make the resin bezel

1. Cut a photo to fit the locket bezel.

2. Mix epoxy (Basics). Apply a light layer of glue to the bezel. Place the photo right-side up and burnish with a craft stick until smooth, taking care to remove any air bubbles (**a**).

3. Let dry completely.

4. Repeat Steps 1–3 with the second photo.

5. Mix epoxy, and glue crystals as desired to frame each photo (**b**).

6. Fill each bezel with embossing powder (**c**). Remove any powder that gets on the sides or outside of the bezel.

7. Follow the manufacturer's directions to set the embossing powder. Heat the locket in a 275° oven until the powder is clear and smooth and the image is visible. Remove from the oven and let cool before handling. If the bezel is not completely full, add more powder and repeat Steps 6–7.

8. Let harden completely (usually 24 hours; however, it takes a few days for the resin to completely harden). Handle carefully.

Add crystals

9. Decorate the locket as desired, using epoxy and crystals (**d**).

Complete the necklace

10. Open a jump ring (Basics), connect an end link of chain and the spring clasp (**e**), and close the jump ring.

11. Attach a jump ring to the end link on the other side.

12. Open a jump ring and attach the locket to the chain. Close the jump ring.

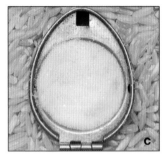

Every oven is different. Experiment with temperatures before starting your final piece. I found that 300° worked better for my oven.

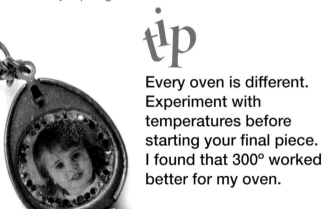

Don't limit yourself to photographs. Small trinkets can be just as appealing and may provide a glimpse into the past.

Amalgamated

Crystals
A variety of color, shapes, and
sizes

Materials
molded filligree pendant
brass filigree pendant (Vintaj
Natural Brass Co., Vintaj.com)
14 x 31mm brass two-hole
Etruscan connector wrap
(Vintaj Natural Brass Co.)
1 in. (2.5cm) head pin
epoxy resin kit
molds
finished ribbon necklace

frame-style pendant
frame or open bezel
rub-on transfer
clear packing tape
Goo Gone
2 feet brass cable chain
2 jump rings
2 5mm brass heishi

Tools
tweezers or wax stick
toothpick
wooden stick
roundnose pliers
2 pairs of chainnose pliers
flush cutters
drill

Bring a mix of materials—crystals, filigree, and graphic images—
together in a unique pendant. There are several construction methods
illustrated here, but all provide the same stunning results.

a

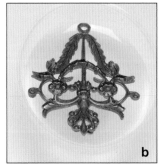

b

Molded filigree pendant
Prepare the filigree
1. Select a filigree pendant that will fit in the mold you want
to use. (Allow some room around all sides of the filigree.
The extra space will make a more pleasing design.)
2. With flush cutters, clip off any loops or parts of the
filigree you want to remove.
3. Plan your crystal pattern pretty side up.
4. Mix epoxy (Basics). Use a toothpick or a syringe to
apply glue to where you want to add crystal. Let glue
set for a few minutes, then add crystals with tweezers or
wax stick (**a**). Dry completely (overnight is best).

Mold the pendant

5. Following manufacturer's directions, completely mix equal parts of resin and hardener (Basics).

6. Fill the mold halfway with the mixed resin. Allow to set undisturbed overnight. (Work on this at the same time you prepare the filigree with crystals.)

7. Slowly pour a thin layer of mixed resin on top of the hardened resin. Slide filigree form into the newly mixed resin (**b**), using a toothpick to push down. After the filigree is secure, completely fill the mold with resin. Pour slowly so you don't cause air bubbles. Set overnight or until resin has fully hardened.

Make the pendant and necklace

8. Drill a small hole through the top of the casting (**c**).

9. Using roundnose pliers, create a bail by bending the Etruscan connector wrap in half (**d**).

10. String a head pin through the front of the bail, the resin casting, and the back of the bail (**e**).

11. Trim the wire to ⅜ in. (1cm) and make a plain loop (Basics, p. 13) (**f**).

12. With chainnose pliers, bend the loop flat against the connector (**g**).

13. String the pendant on a finished ribbon.

Alternative: For an elaborate filigree version, layer the resin but hold back on the final pour so some of the filigree texture is pronounced. Make sure to cover enough of the filigree to secure it.

Frame-style necklace

1. Place a frame or open bezel on a piece of packing tape. Fill halfway with resin and let harden (**h**).

2. Apply a rub-on transfer and glue crystals as desired (**i, j**). When the glue is dry, finish by filling the frame completely with resin and let harden.

3. Remove the frame from the packing tape. Goo Gone will remove any residue.

4. Open a jump ring. String a heishi, a chain end, and one frame loop. Close the jump ring. Repeat on the other side.

c

d

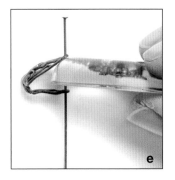

e

f

g

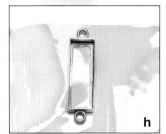

h

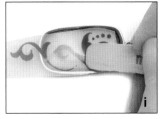

i

j

tip

Save food containers or recycle various types of packaging into a plethora of mold shapes.

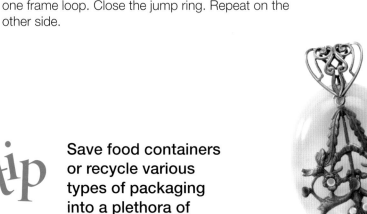

Robin's Egg Blues

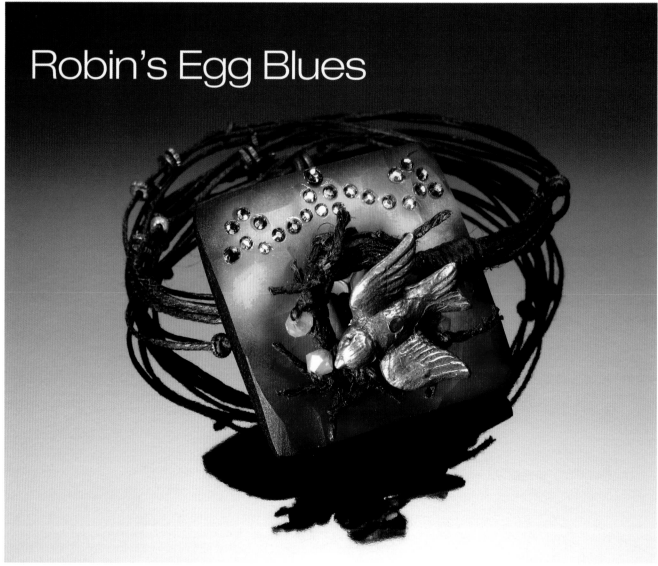

This bitty bird bead called to me, and the nest idea for this bracelet was hatched. Co-designed by Brenda Schweder in her signature style, this crystal egg nursery is built with waxed linen twigs.

Crystals

3 3mm Art. 5000 Pacific Opal
5 SS8 Art. 2028 Black Diamond
18 SS6 Art. 2028 Black Diamond

Materials

6 yds. (5.4m) waxed linen, black
bird bead (Green Girl Studios, greengirlstudios.com)
24 4mm brass heishi
brass head pin
resin donut, olive (Fusion Beads, fusionbeads.com)
G-S Hypo cement
two-part epoxy glue (30 min.)

Tools

big-eye needle
roundnose pliers
chainnose pliers
tweezers
toothpick

1. Mix epoxy (Basics, p. 7). Use a toothpick or a syringe to apply glue to the resin donut where you'd like to add crystals. Add crystals to the face of the donut (**a**). Set aside to dry.

2. String the bird bead on a head pin and make the first half of a wrapped loop underneath the bird (Basics) (**b**).

3. Complete the wrapped loop (Basics). Cut 2 yds. (1.8m) of linen from the total length and set aside. Cut the remaining length in four equal lengths (1 yd./.9m each) and thread them through the loop. Center the bird on the strands and tie in place with an overhand knot (**c**). Tighten the knot to hold the charm in place.

4. Add three heishi to each strand. (The heishi will drift along each strand.)

5. Gather the strands together. Create a loop that will accommodate the bird-as-toggle at the end of the bracelet (calculate your desired finished length, including the loop). Position a big-eyed needle eye-end down along the loop. Start at the juncture of the loop's neck, and coil one strand tightly around the neck of the loop and over the needle, moving downward from the loop (**d**).

6. Pass the end loosely through the needle eye (**e**).

7. Pull the needle through the coil (using a pair of pliers if necessary) until taut. Trim the end close to the coil (**f**) and dot with G-S Hypo cement.

8. Pick up the reserved linen length and cut it into twelve 6-in. (15cm) pieces. Tie 9 of the 12 pieces individually around the linen loop with a double knot (**g**).

9. Tie the remaining pieces around the loop, threading one crystal to each before you knot (**h**). Trim all the linen ends to ¼–½ in. (6–13mm) (**i**).

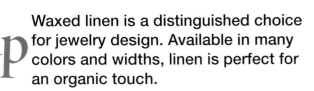

tip Waxed linen is a distinguished choice for jewelry design. Available in many colors and widths, linen is perfect for an organic touch.

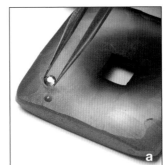

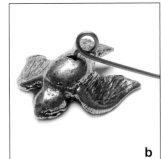

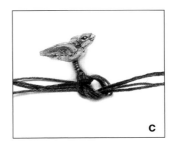

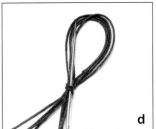

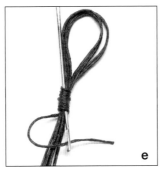

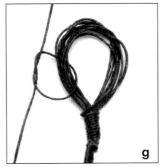

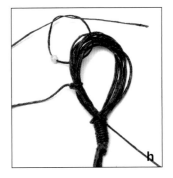

Sitting Pretty

Pinwheels, mesmerizing to children, can be equally fascinating to urbane adults. Take this ring for a spin, and take special note of the colorful crystals.

Crystals (all Art. 2028)
SS10 Pacific Opal
SS6 Pacific Opal

Materials
epoxy resin kit
parchment paper
two-sided decorative paper
interchangeable ring
2 10mm washer spacers
two-part epoxy glue (five min.)

Tools
hole punch
scissors
craft knife
sponge or sponge brush
metal ruler
cutting mat
roundnose pliers
toothpick
syringe (optional)

1. Trace the template onto two-sided paper. Cut out the square and place on parchment paper.

2. Mix two-part resin (Basics). Using a sponge, lightly apply resin to one side of the paper (**a**). Make sure you cover the paper evenly, right to the edge. Turn over and place on fresh parchment. Coat the second side with resin. (You don't have to wait for one side to dry completely before turning over and coating the second. The parchment will keep the cutout from sticking.) Let dry overnight.

3. With scissors or craft knife, trim excess resin and cut lines to the center. Cut notch lines (**b**).

4. Mix two-part epoxy (Basics). Use a toothpick or a syringe to apply glue to one side of washer. Adhere the washer, centering it in the middle of the paper cutout (**c**). Let dry.

5. With hole punch, punch a 1/8-in. (3mm) hole in the center of the cutout. Punch a hole on each of the four corners of the cutout (**d**).

6. Turn over the cutout and repeat Step 4 to adhere a washer to the other side.

7. Using roundnose pliers, curl each point slightly to shape the pinwheel.

8. Mix two-part epoxy. Use a toothpick or a syringe to apply glue where you want to add crystals. Let glue set a little before adding crystals (this will keep them from shifting on the pinwheel).

9. Place the pinwheel on the ring base and screw the top in place (**e**).

tip It is best to work with the resin-coated paper within a few days of drying, since it can become brittle.

a

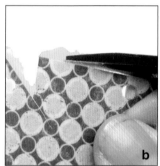
b

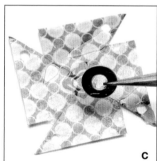
c

d

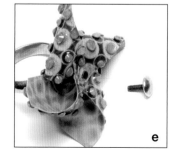
e

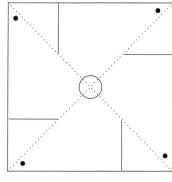
TEMPLATE

All Jeweled

Customize store-bought bangles to make them your own. Don't be afraid to experiment! Resin jewelry is affordable, so you can create to your heart's content.

Version I
Rub-on pattern
1. Using a wooden stick, burnish the rub-on to the bangle in a random pattern (**a**). When complete, spray with matte varnish to protect.
2. Mix epoxy (Basics). With a syringe, apply glue to bangle, adding crystals in a random pattern as you go (**b**).
3. Set aside and let dry completely. (Overnight is best.)

Version II
Paisley pattern
1. Plan your crystal pattern on a flat surface, pretty-side up, using the illustration below as a guide.
2. Mix epoxy (Basics). With a syringe, apply glue where you want the crystals, and place the crystals as you go.
3. Set aside and let dry completely. (Overnight is best.)

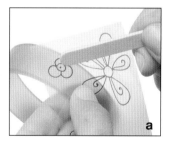

a

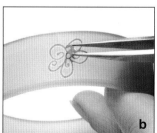

b

Version I Rub-on pattern
Crystals
Art. 2028:
SS16 Pacific Opal
2 SS16 Rose Alabaster
2 SS10 Rose Alabaster
SS12 White Opal
2 SS12 Mint Alabaster
Art. 2080:
SS34 Chalk White AB
SS16 Chalk White
SS16 Sapphire
2 SS 16 Peridot

Materials
resin bangle (Natural Touch Beads, naturaltouchbeads.com)
Making Memories rub-on pattern and wooden stick
spray varnish
two-part epoxy

Version II Paisley pattern
Crystals
a variety of shapes and colors including Palace Green Opal, Topaz, Khaki, Crystal, and Light Gray Opal

Materials
store-bought resin bangle

Tools (both projects)
tweezers
toothpick
syringe

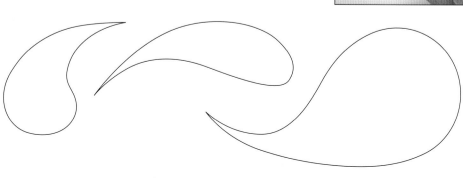

Ring Bling

Play . . . have fun . . . there's no right or wrong way to make these rings. Create random designs, play with color, let the shape lead you, or follow a well-planned pattern. The possibilities abound.

Crystals
Version I
variety of sizes, shapes, colors
Version II (owl)
7 4mm Art. 2400 Copper
2 SS10 Art. 2028 Aquamarine Cosmo Jet
30 SS8 Art. 2028 Jet
75 SS3 Art. 2028 Crystal
Version III (green ring)
28 SS10 Art. 2028 Colorado Topaz
50 SS8 Art. 2028 Aquamarine Cosmo Jet
13 x 8mm Art. 2709 Crystal Copper
Version IV (purple ring)
8 x 14mm Art. 21804 Crystal AB
SS16 Art. 2728 Crystal AB
4 or more SS8 Art. 2028 in Amethyst, Purple Velvet, Topaz
SS5 Art. 2028 Citrine
SS3 Art 2028 Crystal

Materials
variety of store-bought resin rings
two-part epoxy glue (30 min.)

Tools
syringe
tweezers
toothpick

Version I
Random crystal pattern
1. On a flat surface, plan your crystal pattern pretty side up. I used a monochromatic color palette with a square and a smaller round crystal. I played off the existing diamond pattern in the ring.
2. Mix epoxy (Basics). Use a toothpick or syringe to apply glue to the ring (**a**), placing crystals as you go. Repeat until pattern is complete.
3. Set aside to dry completely. (Overnight is best.)

Version II
Owl
1. Follow the pattern and place crystals on a flat surface pretty side up. Use the illustration as a guide.
2. Mix epoxy (Basics). Using a toothpick, start on one end and apply glue to the ring, forming the triangle outline between the eyes. Add Jet crystals around one eye. Add Topaz square at the point of the triangle. Continue adding Jet crystals around the other eye.
3. Set aside and let dry.
4. Mix more glue. Use the toothpick to fill in the triangle shape with glue. Add SS3 crystals, starting with the point. Continue adding rows until the shape is completely filled.
5. Add Aquamarine Cosmo Jet crystals for the eyes.
6. Set aside and let dry.

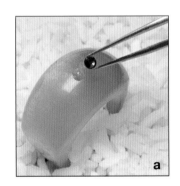

a

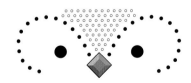

tip

Mall accessory shops and department stores usually carry a great selection of inexpensive resin rings. Part of the fun is the scouting ... you won't believe where these rings pop up.

Fun Stuff

Save the formal wear for **formal** occasions and let your **playful** side show with this **whimsical** and **amusing** jewelry. It's fun to make, but more importantly, it's fun to wear!

Bat and Forth

Cynthia Dies, owner of Ornamentea, designed this great bracelet from a metal bat stamping. I went really batty by adding crystals. Just be careful not to wear it during a full moon!

Crystals (all Art. 2028)
14 SS8 Black Diamond
13 SS3 Crystal

Materials
5 in. (13cm) brass bat stamping
10 in. (25cm) 5–7mm gunmetal thick cable chain
2 brass star charms
9mm brass spring clasp
2 7mm brass jump rings
2 5mm brass jump rings
two-part epoxy glue (5 min.)

Supply note: Bat and all metal findings are from Ornamentea, ornamentea.com

Tools
torch
cup or cylindrical object for mandrel
roundnose pliers
2 pairs of chainnose pliers
tweezers or wax stick
toothpick

Prepare the bat stamping

1. Using a cup as a mandrel, form the stamping around its curve (**a**).

2. Using chainnose pliers, bend the edge of one of the bat wings. Repeat on the other wing (**b**).

3. Using roundnose pliers, form a small loop out of the folded wing tip. Leave enough space to add a 7mm jump ring. Attach the jump ring (Basics) and close the loop (**c**).

4. Use rubber-handled chainnose pliers to hold one end of the bat component over a heat-resistant work surface. Using a butane torch, glide the flame over the component (**d**). (Because metal conducts heat, use caution as it becomes very hot in the oxidizing phase.) Continue to run the flame over the component until the desired look is achieved. (Watch carefully—the effect can change drastically.) Extinguish the flame. Cool completely on a heat-resistant surface.

Make the bracelet

5. Cut two 3-in. (7.6cm) lengths of chain. Open a jump ring and attach a chain segment to one side (**e**). Close the jump ring.

6. Open a 5mm jump ring and attach a spring clasp to the other end of the chain segment. Close the jump ring.

7. Open a 7mm jump ring and attach the other chain segment to the other side of the bat. Close the jump ring.

8. Open a 5mm jump ring and attach metal stars to the end link of chain (**f**). Close the jump rings.

Add crystals

9. Mix epoxy (Basics) and apply a light layer of glue to the body of the bat. Let set and add black diamond crystals to fill body (**g**). Add a line of glue on the wing tips of the bat. Follow the line, placing crystals as you go.

10. Let dry completely.

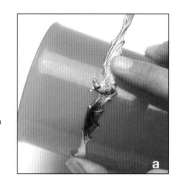

a

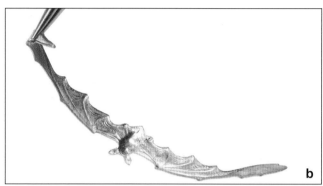

b

c

d

e

tip Different metals can be transformed with different methods. For example, heat colors brass, liver of sulfur can oxidize sterling silver, and ammonia can patinate copper.

f

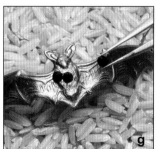

g

Crystal 'Ice'd

Create a winter wonderland out of crystallized snowflake charms. Use a little resourcefulness to find the right bracelet platform to showcase the snowflakes.

Crystals

Snowflake 1
2 10mm Art. 2493, chessboard Crystal Silver Shade
12 SS10 Art. 2028, Crystal Silver Shade

Snowflake 2
2 SS16 Art. 2728, Crystal AB
16 SS5 Art. 2028, Crystal AB

Snowflake 3
12 SS5 Art. 2028, Crystal AB
2 SS10 Art. 2028, Crystal Silver Shade

Snowflake 4
2 8 x 4mm Art. 2180/4, Crystal
12 SS5 Art. 2028, Crystal AB
12 SS3 Art. 2028, Crystal
12 SS8 Art. 2028, Crystal Silver Shade

Snowflake 5
10 SS12 Art. 2028, White Opal
2 SS16 Art. 2080, Crystal AB
12 SS5 Art. 2028, Crystal AB

Snowflake 6
8 5 x 2.8mm Art. 2510, Crystal

Snowflake 7
2 SS16 Art. 2728, Crystal
16 SS3 Art. 2000, Crystal

Materials
purchased charm bracelet
2 each of 7 assorted charms
7 7mm silver bails or jump rings
two-part epoxy glue (5 min.)

Tools
tweezers
two pairs of chainnose pliers
toothpick
syringe (optional)

Prepare the charms

1. Divide the charms into matching sets of two. Mix epoxy (Basics). Use a toothpick to apply glue to the back of one charm and adhere it to its match (**a**). Let dry.

Add crystals

2. Set crystals on your work surface pretty side up (**b**).
3. Mix epoxy (Basics). Use a toothpick or a syringe to apply glue where you want to add crystals on one side of the snowflake. Add crystals (**c**). Repeat for all charms. Set aside to dry.
4. Mix more two-part epoxy. Use either a toothpick or a syringe to apply glue to the other side of the snowflake to duplicate the crystal pattern on the reverse. Repeat for all charms. Set aside to dry.

Finish the bracelet

5. Add a bail or jump ring (Basics) to the charms (**d**) and attach them to a store-bought charm bracelet.

tip

Gluing symmetrical charms back-to-back adds a nice finishing touch. No matter how the charm hangs, the pretty side is always showing.

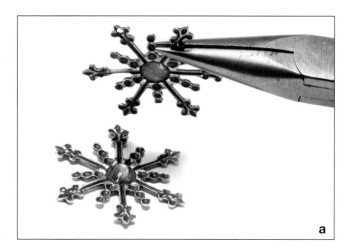

a

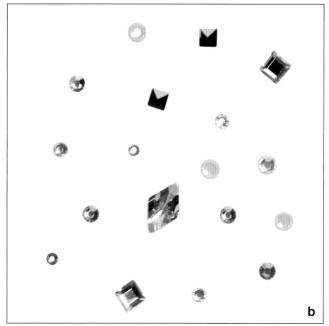

b

c

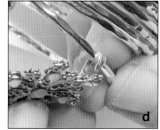

d

It's Not a Dog's Life

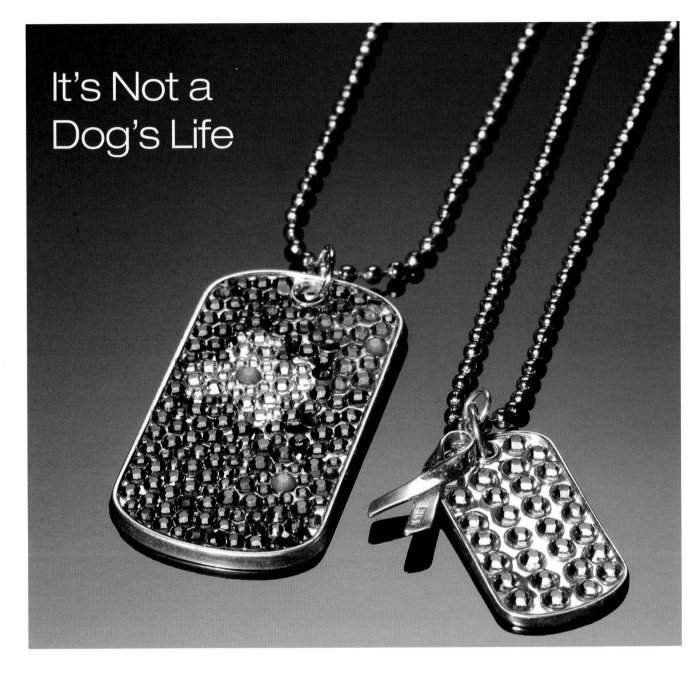

It's your life! Showcase your originality with a custom version of the conventional dog tag.

Crystals (all Art. 2028)
Version I
SS10 Rose

Version II
SS10 Caribbean Blue
SS10 Ruby
SS6 Ruby
SS10 Hyacinth
SS6 Hyacinth
SS10 Jonquil
SS6 Citrine
SS6 Amethyst
SS6 Purple Velvet

Materials
49.6 x 27.8mm silver
    rectangular dog tag
breast cancer charm (version I)
24 in. (61cm) 2mm silver ball
    chain
clear contact paper
5mm silver jump rings
two-part epoxy glue (30 min.)

Tools
2 pairs chainnose pliers
tweezers or wax stick
toothpick

Version I
Breast cancer awareness

1. Mix epoxy (Basics, p. 7). Use a toothpick to fill the bezel with a thin layer of glue. Add a row of crystals at the edge of the bezel (**a**). Add a second row directly below the first. Continue adding rows until the bezel is completely filled. (Work quickly to fill the entire bezel before the glue sets.) Set aside to dry.

Version II
Flowers

1. Mix epoxy (Basics). Use a toothpick or syringe to apply glue to where you want to add crystals. Begin one of the flowers by adding a Caribbean Blue crystal for the center. Working your way out, develop the Hyacinth crystal flower. Add the other two flowers in Ruby, Jonquil, and Citrine crystals.

2. Fill the remaining bezel with a thin layer of glue and apply crystals to completely fill the tag. Alternate the sizes to fill completely. Set aside to dry.

Finish the necklace

1. Open a jump ring (Basics), and attach the tag and the charm (Version I only) to the chain (**b**). Close the jump ring.

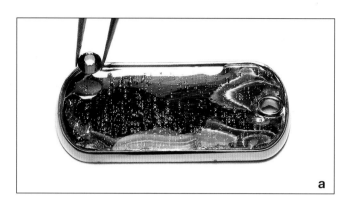

a

b

 tip

Add an additional element, like a charm or shell.

Let Go of My Lego

These clever cuff links bring new life to a box of forgotten building blocks. Aren't there some fashion doll accessories that need a crystal lift as well?

Crystals (all Art. 2028)
8 SS16 Chalk White
4 SS16 Grey Opal
4 SS16 Jet Hematite

Materials
assorted Lego blocks in sets of two
cuff-link findings
two-part epoxy (5 min.)

Tools
toothpicks
tweezers

Embellish the blocks

1. Mix epoxy (Basics). Use toothpick to apply glue to the back of a small toy piece. Attach one or two small pieces to the top of a larger base piece (**a**). Set aside to dry.

2. Mix epoxy. Use a toothpick or a syringe to apply glue where you want to add crystals. Add crystals (**b**). Set aside to dry.

3. Make a matching set.

Assemble cuff link

4. Mix epoxy. Using a toothpick, apply glue to the back of the cuff link finding. Adhere the finding to the center of the back of the unit (**c**). Set aside to dry.

5. Repeat to make a second cuff link.

Alternative charms

Plastic doll accessories (embellished with crystals) make great charms. Revisit your childhood and play with these little gems. You'll need a drill, some jump rings, epoxy, and, of course, some crystals.

1. Choose several plastic accessories and drill holes with a ⅜-in. bit (**d**).

2. Open a jump ring (Basics) and attach it to the charm (**e**). Close the jump ring.

3. Mix epoxy (Basics). Using a toothpick, apply glue to the charm where you want to add crystals. Place crystals (**f**) until you are happy with the design. Set aside to dry.

4. Open a jump ring and attach to your favorite charm bracelet. Close the jump ring.

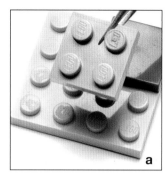

a

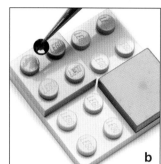

b

c

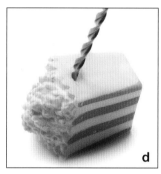

d

e

f

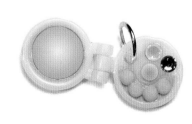

Lucky Charms

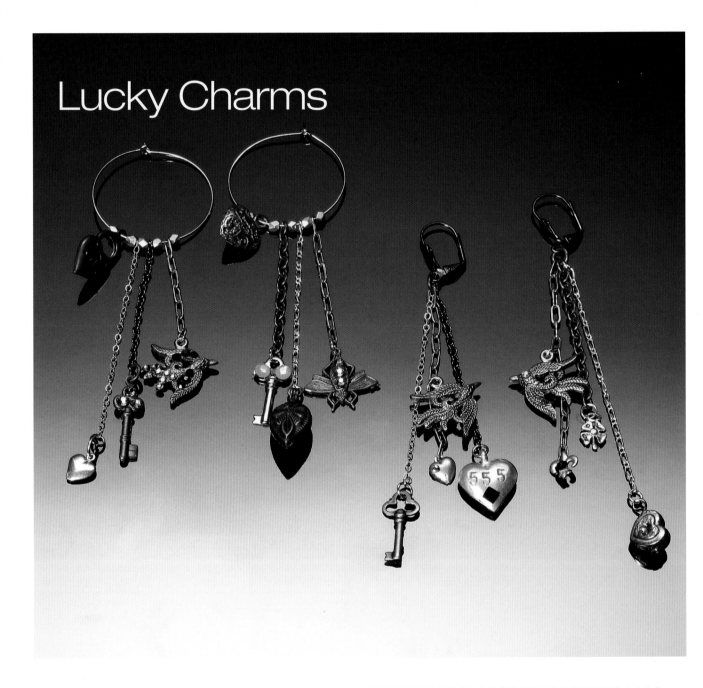

Fashion these magically intriguing charms into earrings. Just add them to lengths of chain for a one of-a-kind creation.

tip Select charms with dimension on all sides, because the fronts and backs will be visible as they dangle.

Crystals
Variety of sizes, shapes, and colors

Materials
variety of charms
variety of 1mm and 2mm link chain in several finishes
6–10 3mm jump rings
pair of gunmetal earring findings or a pair of brass earring hoops
2mm brass spacers
two-part epoxy (5 min.)

Tools
roundnose pliers
2 pairs chainnose pliers
tweezers or wax stick
toothpick

Add crystals

1. Mix epoxy (Basics). Apply glue to charms and decorate all sides with crystals (**a**). Set aside to dry.

Add charms to chain

2. Cut varying lengths of chain.

3. Open a jump ring (Basics), and attach a charm to a chain segment (**b**). Close the jump ring. (Jump rings in a thin gauge work well with small chain.)

4. For charms without a loop, mix epoxy and use a toothpick to apply epoxy to the back of the charm. Carefully place the chain end in the glue (**c**). If the chain is small enough, I like to glue a matching charm to the other side, like a sandwich.

5. Open a jump ring and attach all chains and an earring finding (**d**). Close the jump ring.

6. Repeat Steps 1–5 to make a second earring.

Create a different look by adding chain to a loop earring instead

1. Follow Steps 1–4 above to make charms and hang them from chain.

2. String a 2mm brass spacer on the earring loop. Add a charm to the earring loop. Alternate spacers and chain units (**e**). Finish with a 2mm spacer.

3. Using chainnose pliers, slightly bend the back of the earring loop (**f**).

4. Repeat Steps 1–3 to make a second earring.

a

b

c

d

tip Don't be afraid to mix different finishes of chain. I used silver, brass, and gunmetal finishes.

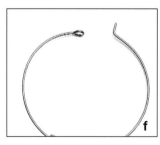

f

e

note: Charms and charm bracelets can be traced back as early as 5,000 B.C. Ancient Egyptians used various charms to protect them from a variety of evil forces. Early Christians wore symbolic charms for protection or good luck. Queen Victoria wore a charm bracelet of small lockets containing photographs of her family. Shortly after, charm bracelets became the must-have accessory, and they still make a strong showing in fashion today.

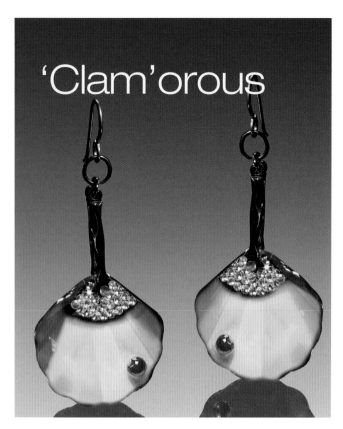

'Clam'orous

Layer crystals upon crystals—and accent with yet another crystal—for elegant earrings.

Crystals
2 28mm Art. 6723 pendant, Crystal Golden Shadow
32 SS3 Art. 2028, Crystal
2 SS16 Art. 2084, Jet

Materials
4 links gunmetal 2mm bar-and-loop chain
2 2-in. (5cm) brass or gunmetal head pins
2 gunmetal ear wires
two-part epoxy glue (5 min.)

Tools
roundnose pliers
2 pairs chainnose pliers
tweezers or wax stick
toothpick

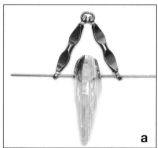
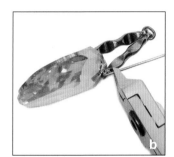
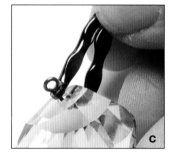

Make earrings
1. Fold the bar-and-loop chain segment in half so a bar hangs on each side of the loop. String a head pin through the hole in a bar segment, the crystal pendant (from the decorative side), and the other bar (**a**).
2. Trim the head pin to ⅜ in. (1cm) (**b**) and make a plain loop (Basics) (**c**). With chainnose pliers, bend the loop against the pendant (**d**).
3. Open an earring wire and attach the center ring of chain (**e**). Close the earring wire.
4. Repeat Steps 1-3 to make a second earring.

Add crystals
5. Mix epoxy (Basics). Use a toothpick to apply glue to the pendant where you want to add crystals, and place the crystals (**f**). Set aside to dry. Repeat with the second earring.

Small pendants of any shape can be transformed into a pair of earrings and embellished with extra crystals.

Gallery

The Gallery shows what can happen when you let loose and play. It's a place to experiment and to try anything. Let this work inspire you and just have fun!

Fashionista's Prize

2008 Debbi Simon

Resin-coated paper, crystals. Inspired by a paper doll book and a closet full of fashion.

Decouper

2008 Debbi Simon

Torn paper, lacquer, crystals. This piece employs the basics of decoupage; torn paper applied to a plain resin bangle with several coats of protective lacquer and decorated with crystals.

Off the Cuff

2007 Debbi Simon

Leather and crystals. The large crystals enhance this leather cuff and create a juxtaposition of textures.

Dragonfly Purse

2007 Kristal Wick

Silk, gemstones, crystals. The edges of the purse, dragonflies, and Sassy Silkies scroll beads are accented with a variety of flat-back crystals, adding even more texture to the piece. Another surprise is how the flat-back crystals pick up the metallic colors in the hand-painted silk used for this purse.

Rolodex Among Friends

2008
Madison Simon
Meagan Grass
Geena Grass

Gift cards, crystals, and beads. A favorite kids'-class activity was to make Artist Trading Cards. This project takes it to the next level, converting the cards into a bracelet.

Fender

2008 Debbi Simon

Guitar picks, crystals, guitar strings, brass. Crystal accents on Fender guitar picks create a piece that is kitschy with a dash of rock'n'roll. What better finish than to complete the necklace with real guitar strings?

Crystal
Masquerade

2007 Lisa Pavelka

Gallery Finalist 4th place
CREATE YOUR STYLE
with CRYSTALLIZED™
– *Swarovski Elements*
2007 Design Contest

Polymer clay and crystals.
Flatbacks of varying sizes
and shapes and lots of
Zillion Rose were set into
polymer clay to make this
magnificent mask.

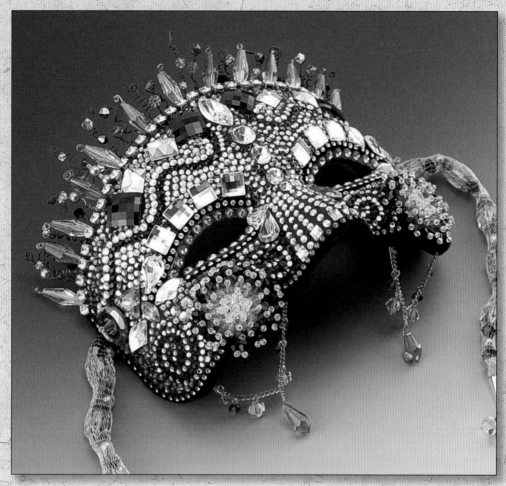

Memory of
Grandmother

2008
Brenda Schweder and
Debbi Simon

Crystals, head pins, fiber. This
piece evolved by merging Debbi's
grandmother's relic with Brenda's way
with vintage objects. Attention to detail,
such as the metal embellishment on the
large crystals, the adorned photo inside
the compact, and the crystal detail on the
tassel makes this piece unique.

Relique

2008 Kristal Wick

Metal, crystals, beads. Flat-back crystals enhance the ancient-looking patinated charms, creating a contrast of bright and aged and resulting in a melding of new and old worlds.

Faux

2008 Debbi Simon

Faux bone, crystals, paint, wax. Faux Bone is a new material for jewelry making that can be sanded, molded, stamped, drilled, and carved. The medium is further embellished with crystals and an encaustic painting technique favored by the artist.

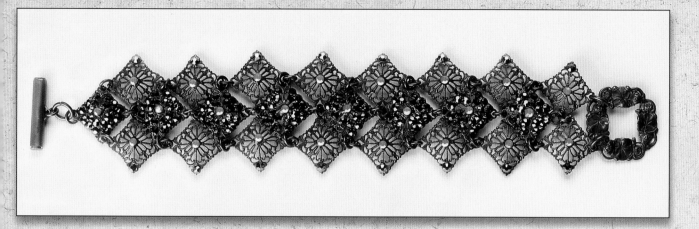

Linked

2007 Debbi Simon

Stamped filigree, flat-back crystals. Inspired by the Victorian era, this bracelet was the inspiration for this book.

Betty Boop

2008 Roxie Moede

Resin, crystals. Simple can be better. Just because you can glue lots of crystals on anything doesn't mean you should. Take Betty Boop. A few red crystal accents is all she needs.

Layered

2007 Debbi Simon

Filligree, crystals. Layered pieces of filigree with subtle crystal accents create a focal point for this necklace.

Lap Turtle

2006 Kellie DeFries
Gallery Finalist 3rd place
CREATE YOUR STYLE with CRYSTALLIZED™
– Swarovski Elements 2006 Design Contest

Computer, crystals. Kellie is a graduate of McNeese State University with a B.A. degree in both ceramics and graphic design. Her use of color and simplicity of form are an essential part of her design expression.

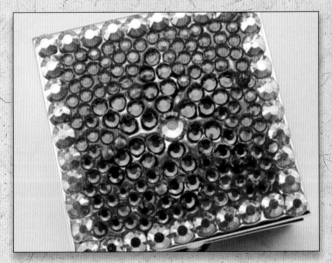

Floral Sparkle Pill Box

2007 Lisa Pavelka

Pill box, crystals. The crystals create a great statement and fashion accessory. Lisa Pavelka is an award-winning artist and author who specializes in combining polymer clay with other media such as crystals, metal clays, wire, and more.

Acknowledgments

I'd like to thank CREATE YOUR STYLE with CRYSTALLIZED™ – *Swarovski Elements* for providing both crystals and technical support for this book. Rebecca has become a friend and my go-to resource … thank you. Nicole had the daunting task of filling my orders. Your smile travels over phone lines and through the computer. You have helped make this book beautiful.

I was honored to work with the "best of the best" to make the projects for this book. My thanks go to Beadalon, Becky Nunn Designs, Blue Mud, Frost Creek Charms, Jewels n Findings, J.P. Designs, Ornamenta, Patera, Rio Grande, Shiana, Susan Lenart Kazmer, and Vintaj Natural Brass Co.

Of course thanks to my children, Madison and Dominic, or Dominic and Madison—how best to write this so they both get a chance at being first?—who weathered the destruction writing a book leaves behind. We have the kitchen and dining room tables back … for now!

I love you both more than anything and am proud of the young adults you are becoming.

Special thanks to my wonderful friend Brenda, whose effortless way with words made *Crystal Chic* so much more interesting and fun to read. Without your input and support, this book couldn't be what it is; you truly are my artist alter ego. I look forward to many more projects with you.

A final word of thanks to everyone else— my family and all my amazing friends. I am blessed with lots of remarkable people in my life whose love, support, and most of all, encouragement have helped me grow as a person and an artist. I have learned to take risks and take on new challenges—this being the biggest so far. This includes all my fellow Kalmbach coworkers. I would like to thank Kalmbach Publishing Co. for giving me many great opportunities.

Debbi Simon has worked with a variety of art mediums and subject matter over the years. Since 1993, her paintings have been exhibited in juried and invitational shows, and group and solo regional exhibitions throughout the Midwest. She has won numerous awards for her paintings. Her original jewelry designs have been featured in *Bead&Button* and *BeadStyle* magazines.

Debbi studied art and design at the Milwaukee Institute of Art & Design, earning a BFA in design with a minor in illustration and photography. She continually experiments with new media. An introduction to beads through her day job—advertising sales for Kalmbach's bead titles—added jewelry making to her mix.

Debbi has developed art workshops for both children and adults, and she has taught classes at the Bead&Button Show and seminars for Swarovski.

"Teaching adult classes helps me connect with other creative people," says Debbi, "and the children's classes allow me to share my art with my own children and their friends. I wish we all could all go back and create with the refreshing innocence of a child … without preconceived ideas and with pride in the final work."

"My use of different colors and finishes is what defines my signature style. An art teacher once said that my strength was my use of color. I didn't understand this at the time. And to be honest, I still don't. When I try to apply the formal theories and rules of color to my designs, they hold me back. I have learned to just go with my gut, and happily, it seems to work! "

All in the Family

My children couldn't be more different as artists, but they both could tell you that blue and yellow make green, red and yellow make orange, and so on before they entered kindergarten (my greatest achievement). Here are their contributions to my book.

Pez Series:
- Pez Belle, 2008, Madison Simon
- Pez Nemo, 2008, Dominic Simon

Create
beautiful beaded jewelry
with this series

Creative Beading
The best projects from a year of Bead&Button magazine
62288

Creative Beading Vol. 2
The best projects from a year of Bead&Button magazine
62441

Creative Beading Vol. 3
The best projects from a year of Bead&Button magazine
62625

$29.95 each

Spark your creativity with the wide variety of jewelry designs in every hardcover volume of *Creative Beading*. You'll find thorough Basics sections and inspiring projects grouped by technique, including bead embroidery and crocheting, stringing, wirework, and more. You'll also discover the fantastic stitching projects *Bead&Button* magazine is famous for. Make creative beaded jewelry to wear or share in no time!

**Order online at
www.BeadAndCraftBooks.com
or call 1-800-533-6644**

Monday – Friday, 8:30 a.m. – 5:00 p.m. Central Time.
Outside the U.S. and Canada, call 262-796-8776, ext. 661.

KB
KALMBACH BOOKS

PMK-BKS-62694RH

XB